Uwe Hartmann

War without Fighting?

The Reintegration of Former Combatants in Afghanistan seen through the Lens of Strategic Thought

War without Fighting?

The Reintegration of Former Combatants in Afghanistan seen through the Lens of Strategic Thought

Uwe Hartmann

2014

Carola Hartmann Miles-Verlag

CIP-Kurztitelaufnahme der Deutschen Nationalbibliothek

Uwe Hartmann:
War without Fighting? The Reintegration of Former Combatants in
Afghanistan seen through the Lens of Strategic Thought

Carola Hartmann Miles-Verlag, Berlin 2014
ISBN 978-3-937885-86-5

Titelbild: ISAF HQ Kabul; Regional Command North Masar-e
Sharif

Herstellung: Books on Demand, Norderstedt

© Carola Hartmann Miles-Verlag,
George-Caylay-Str. 38, 14089 Berlin
(email: Miles-Verlag@t-online.de;
www.miles-verlag.jimdo.com)

Printed in Germany

ISBN 978-3-937885-86-5

Table of Content

Securing peace and an end to fighting are the most significant demands of our people. For the last thirty years, our people have offered continuous sacrifices to achieve peace. It is a recognized fact that security and peace cannot be achieved through fighting and violence. This is why the Islamic Republic of Afghanistan has placed national reconciliation at the top of its peace-building policy. We welcome and will provide necessary help to all disenchanted compatriots who are willing to return to their homes, live peacefully and accept the Constitution. We invite dissatisfied compatriots, who are not directly linked to international terrorism, to return to their homeland.

President Karsai, Inauguration Speech

November 19, 2009

Four score and seven years ago our fathers brought forth on this continent, a new nation, conceived in Liberty, and dedicated to the proposition that all men are created equal.

Now we are engaged in a great civil war, testing whether that nation, or any nation so conceived and so dedicated, can long endure. We are met on a great battlefield of that war. We have come to dedicate a portion of that field, as a final resting place for those who here gave their lives that that nation might live. It is altogether fitting and proper that we should do this.

But, in a larger sense, we can not dedicate—we can not consecrate—we can not hallow—this ground. The brave men, living and dead, who struggled here, have consecrated it, far above our poor power to add or detract. The world will little note, nor long remember what we say here, but it can never forget what they did here. It is for us the living, rather, to be dedicated here to the unfinished work which they who fought here have thus far so nobly advanced. It is rather for us to be here dedicated to the great task remaining before us—that from these honored dead we take increased devotion to that cause for which they gave the last full measure of devotion—that we here highly resolve that these dead shall not have died in vain—that this nation, under God, shall have a new birth of freedom—and that government of the people, by the people, for the people, shall not perish from the earth.

Abraham Lincoln, Gettysburg Address

November 19, 1863

1   Introduction

War is commonly understood as an extremely violent human interaction. However, warfare may incorporate ways that serve the overall political objectives by predominately using non-violent means. Reintegration belongs to these ways.

"Reintegration is the process by which ex-combatants acquire civilian status and gain sustainable employment and income."[1] Through this process, they lay down their weapons, swear allegiance to the new government, and again become honorable members of communities.

From a conceptual point of view, reintegration is the third step following disarmament and demobilization efforts. Most often, Disarmament, Demobilization, and Reintegration (DDR) programs have been launched after the belligerent parties have officially declared the end of the fighting. As the UN guidelines on DDR state, "The objective of the DDR process is to contribute to security and stability *in post-conflict process* (highlighted by U.H.) with political, military, security, humanitarian and socio-economic dimensions."[2]

However, in Afghanistan, it is different. Realizing that DDR in the first years of the international military presence had achieved limited successes only, President Karsai introduced a new program called the Afghan Peace and Reconciliation Program (APRP) in 2010. It has offered insurgents the opportunity to reintegrate in civil society at a time when the fighting between the Taliban on the one side and the Afghan National Security Forces (ANSF) with ISAF in support on the other side has reached its climax of intensity.

Launching reintegration in the midst of a conflict is a bold political decision. British Major General Phil Jones stressed that the Afghan and coalition leaders had to "overcome incredible scepticism

---

[1] United Nations Inter-agency Working Group on Disarmament, Demobilization and Reintegration, *Operational Guide to the Integrated Disarmament, Demobilization and Reintegration Standards*, 2010, 25.

[2] *Ibid.*, 24; see also ADRP 3-07 *Stability*, Headquarters, Department of the Army, August 2012.

and doubt that a social peace program could emerge in the middle of this conflict."[3] So far, more than 7,000 combatants have been reintegrated, meaning approximately every fourth or fifth fighter. Due to the successes that have been achieved by the APRP, this innovative approach may challenge the traditional DDR concepts.[4]

Referencing DDR experiences from other countries and DDR programs in Afghanistan, this book examines the lessons learned that have been incorporated in the APRP. As in other countries, Afghanistan will be facing the challenges of reintegration for many years to come. This requires not only the long-term financial commitment of the International Community (IC), but also the consistent political will of the Afghan government, the continuous improvement of administrative capacities, constant support provided by the security institutions, and the enduring commitment of the people to live together with former adversaries.

This book continues with the examination of the strategic implications of reintegration in wartime. What intellectual concepts and tools do theories of war and strategy contain to better understand reintegration?[5] The primacy of policies, war as a paradoxical trinity, peace as the ultimate objective of war, the impact of culture on strategies, and the concept of limited war are propositions of strategic thought that critically enlighten the phenomenon of reintegration in times of war. It becomes evident that reintegration should not be seen as the sole realm of counterinsurgency (COIN). By contrast, reintegration must be regarded as an essential, even supreme element in the development of strategies.

Reintegration may not be suitable for all future conflicts. Nevertheless, the assessment of the feasibility, acceptability, and suitability of reintegration should not start when a conflict fought with

---

[3] Quoted in Lisa Daniel, "Reintegration builds confidence in Afghanistan," *American Forces Press Service*, 19 September 2011. Major General Phil Jones was the first Director of Force Reintegration Cell (FRIC).

[4] It needs to be noted that reintegration was also conducted at the peak of the Vietnam War. See Seth G. Jones, "Reintegrating Afghan Insurgents", *Occasional Paper RAND National Defense Research Institute*, 2011, 19.

[5] The use of the word 'strategy' follows the definition of Colin S. Gray as "the use or threat of military power for political purposes". See Colin S. Gray, *On Strategy*, Oxford (University Press) 1999, 15.

military means is close to termination but rather as soon as possible after the initial outbreak of hostilities. If reintegration is launched in the midst of a conflict, all strategic leaders must be aware that this will likely have a significant impact on their strategies. Ends, ways and means must be adjusted to better support the political purposes of reintegration programs. Reintegration must also be considered in the restructuring of headquarters and forces, and of the professional education system.

However, strategists should be aware that reintegration cannot replace the use or threat of violence. Reintegration is not a panacea for subduing the enemy without fighting, a concept which Sun Tzu defined as the acme of skill.[6] The capability of the host country and the intervention forces to fight successfully and the perceptions of the people are often decisive in the insurgent's willingness to reintegrate. Consequently, the utility of force should shape the support of reintegration, wherever possible and to the greatest extent possible.

This principle should have an impact on the conduct of military operations as well as on the whole-of-government approach. In its last chapters, this book offers proposals on how to design military operations and how to improve the civil-military cooperation in order to enhance the unity of efforts in supporting the reintegration initiatives of host nations in conflict areas.

---

[6] Sun Tzu, *The Art of War*, London/Oxford/New York (Oxford University Press) 1971, 77.

2   Reintegration – General Insights

Reintegration should be understood in a broad context, as British staff officer John Alexander instructs: "Social reintegration linking disarmament, demobilization and reintegration (DDR) programmes with transitional justice and reconciliation is widely seen as the most successful and enduring form, with the UN identifying social reintegration of former combatants as the ultimate objective."[7] Consequently, sustained reintegration of former combatants must have a legal or moral basis, accepted by government authorities and the populace, thereby bolstering the peace process.

DDR programs have been executed in several countries predominantly in Africa, Asia and South America, resulting in an extensive body of research.[8] This research emphasizes the difficult decisions with no clear-cut answers that governments and DDR officials nevertheless have to make.

Legality or Reconciliation?

Should insurgents be granted a blanket amnesty, should they be handed over to the national or international justice system for trial, should a reconciliation process at a local level be established or should a mixture of all three apply?

In accordance with international law, individuals who have committed war crimes must be brought to justice. Failing or failed states, sometimes even developing states, do not possess sufficient legal capacities to try all those who committed atrocities and human rights violations below the threshold of war crimes. If these states decide to bind reintegration with transitional justice, they may over-

---

[7] John Alexander, "Decomposing an Insurgency. Reintegration in Afghanistan", *RUSI Journal*, August/September 2012, vol. 157, no. 4, 58. John Alexander is a RAF Regiment Officer. He worked as Chief of Staff FRIC, ISAF Headquarters, from June 2011 till June 2012.

[8] Lessons learned can be drawn on different levels of analysis: the individual, the state, and the international system. See Joseph S. Nye, Jr., David A. Welch, *Understanding Global Conflict and Cooperation. An Introduction to Theory and History*, Boston (Longman) 2011, 46-55.

12

tax their judicial systems.[9] If states forego prosecuting war criminals so that reconciliation does not stall, then different approaches are possible, ranging from national peace and truth commissions to reconciliation efforts on a local level. Examples are South-Africa at the end of the Apartheid regime or Rwanda after 1994, where the accountability for the genocide was followed by the national judicial system in only a few significant cases while the majority of cases were handed over to the village communities.

The government's decision on the most suitable approach is not only dependent on the state's capacities but also on the country's culture. Local reconciliation requires attitudes and values that may not favor state intervention but rather traditional institutions in local communities, and that emphasize forgiveness. Indeed, this approach may undermine the state's authority.[10] However, if the legal system is still nascent and the state's institutions suffer from acceptance by the people, relying on local cultural traditions of conflict resolution is more suitable to the successful conduct of reintegration.

Underlying Causes of War

Social reintegration requires that the underlying causes of war be addressed. This is a very complicated matter for all stakeholders involved. Conflict resolution becomes even more difficult if grievances with government authorities cannot be discussed and resolved, and atrocities committed during the conflict may exacerbate feelings of injustice among the populace. In addition, the suboptimal execution of the reintegration program may generate new grievances.

Long Term Process

Reintegration is a long lasting process, in particular in the case of the non-legal approach. It does not end with the reintegration ceremony conducted by the inhabitants of a village. Transition payments, voca-

---

[9] This was the case in Colombia. See Jonathan Morgenstein, "Consolidating Disarmament. Lessons from Colombia's Reintegration Program for Demobilized Paramilitaries", *United States Institute for Peace,* Special Report 217, Nov 2008, 1.

[10] From the state's perspective, justice procedures and law enforcement mechanisms that are accepted by the former insurgents as well as by the communities would demonstrate its legitimacy and power.

tional training, formal schooling, and psychosocial counseling are obligatory elements of the reintegration process[11]. These supporting DDR programs are rarely implemented fully due to time and budget constraints.

Moreover, poor economic development often affords little opportunity for former combatants to find employment. Analysts Andrea Tamagnini and Theresa Kraft conclude in their study on reintegration in Liberia: "The experience with DDRR (Disarmament, Demobilization, Rehabilitation and Reintegration; U.H.) in Liberia shows that a targeted assistance program may help with the immediate reintegration of ex-combatants. Nevertheless, long-term reintegration of ex-combatants and other war-affected populations is highly dependent on the availability of alternative livelihood. Faced with the absence of employment opportunities in a postwar economy, reintegration programs are under pressure to find short- and medium-term solutions in order to stabilize the situation until long-term economic recovery shows its effects." [12] In Mozambique, reintegration has remained an unresolved affair, although the civil war ended more than 20 years ago. In this country, the government had to again launch a program to ease the living conditions of reintegrated former combatants.[13] If former combatants perceive themselves as disadvantaged, and if the insurgency is ongoing or again on the brink, they may rejoin insurgent groups, or, at least, advise others to fight the government. They may also become engaged in illegal activities to generate income.[14] Consequently, mechanisms must be established to monitor potential discontent and to act swiftly.

---

[11] See "USAID to fund reintegration of former fighters to society," *Colombo Times*, Oct 30, 2009. See also Andrea Tamagnin, Teresa Krafft, "Strategic Approaches to Reintegration: Lessons Learned from Liberia," *Global Governance* 16 (2010), 15.

[12] Tamagnini/Kraft, "Strategic Approaches to Reintegration, 16, 13.

[13] Nelson Alusala, Dominique Dye, "Reintegration in Mozambique. An unresolved affair," *ISS Paper* 217, September 2010.

[14] Prosper Nzekani Zena, "The Lessons and Limits of DDR in Africa," *African Security Brief*, No 24 (Africa Center for Strategic Studies), January 2013.

Communities are Targets, too

Broad consensus exists among theorists and practitioners that both reintegrating individuals and their new communities must benefit from reintegration. Analysts Nelson Alusala and Dominique Dye conclude, "As many community members may also be unemployed after wars and conflicts, they may well resent ex-combatants receiving 'special attention' in acquiring employment. Reintegration interventions should therefore be designed and implemented in such a way that they benefit entire communities, as opposed to individuals."[15] Reintegration can only be successful, if communities take an active part in helping former combatants reintegrate. Consequently, development projects should encourage and subsidize reintegration programs in affected communities.

Difficult Administration

The support of former combatants and the receiving communities requires a comprehensive and effective administration.[16] If the processes are not administered properly, former combatants may consider a return to their former life as fighters. In order to achieve unity of effort and to prevent any sectarian intervention that favors specific ethnicities or religious groups, the administration of reintegration should be controlled by agencies of the central government that are held accountable for allocating the available resources. However, the principle of subsidiarity must apply, and the administrative procedures must be flexible enough to allow adaptation to local needs.[17]

This requires close cooperation between the different levels of government as well as with the international organizations involved. The latter are requested to establish a regime to control the flow of budgets without burdening the processes by bureaucratic overload. Too strict procedures may limit the flexibility that the local authorities need to meet the requirements as identified within com-

---

[15] Alusala/Dye, "Reintegration in Mozambique, 8-10.
[16] Macartan Humphreys, Jeremy Weinstein, "Demobilization and Reintegration", *The Journal of Conflict Resolution*, Vol. 51, no. 4 (Aug. 2007), 12.
[17] Morgenstein, "Consolidating Disarmament," 6.

munities.[18] Staff personnel must be highly educated in the government's and the international organizations' policies and procedures on reintegration, particularly in how to request and approve resources available for the demobilized individuals and their communities.[19]

Information is Key

All stakeholders must read, understand, and deliberate on the reintegration strategy, meaning that ends, ways, and means must be addressed. Information is important, especially when the administrative procedures suffer from friction and intrusive political intervention. Information sharing includes, among others, active as well as former insurgents, their families and tribes, the communities, the officials in the administration, and the personnel of the security organizations (including the intervention forces). Otherwise, unrealistic expectations, misunderstandings, contradictory activities and, as a consequence, new grievances will undermine the reintegration process.[20]

Specific Persons need special Treatment

Within insurgents groups, specific persons must be given special attention. Among those, leaders are valuable targets for outreach, because they may bring members of their groups with them. Since leaders have to give up social prestige, income and power in reintegrating, it might be necessary to offer them equivalent positions within the state structure. Former insurgents who were traumatized by experienced violence need extended counseling. Child soldiers and women must also be treated with specific programs.[21]

---

[18] The United Nations Development Program (UNDP) plays a major role in reintegration as a trust fund (e.g. in Liberia and in Afghanistan).

[19] See Morgenstein, "Consolidating Disarmament," 2; Zena, "The Lessons and Limits of DDR in Africa," 7.

[20] Morgenstein, "Consolidating Disarmament," 2.

[21] *Operational Guide to the Integrated Disarmament, Demobilization and Reintegration Standards*, New York 2010, 193-222. See also Alpaslan Özerdem, Sukanya Podder (eds.), *Child soldiers: from recruitment to reintegration*, Palgrave Macmillan 2011; Jeannie Annan, Christopher Blattman, Dyan Mazurana, Khristopher Carlson, "Civil war,

16

To sum up, general insights on reintegration are available that may serve as guidelines for the development of future programs. Their chances of success increase if they are tailored to the country's specific political, cultural and economic characteristics. Finally, as Nelson Alusala and Dominique Dye, based on their research in Africa, conclude: "Helping ex-combatants reintegrate into society, socially and economically, has long been recognized as a lengthy and complex process, fraught with challenges."[22]

Reintegration, and Gender in Northern Uganda," *Journal of Conflict Resolution*, 2011, 1-32.

[22] Alusala/Dye, "Reintegration in Mozambique," 2.

3   Afghan Peace and Reintegration Program

President Karsai announced the launch of the Afghan Peace and Reintegration Program (APRP) at his inauguration speech on November 19, 2009, targeting the non-ideologically driven fighters and low- to mid-level commanders.[23] Later, he said in an interview with the German magazine *Der Spiegel*: "The reintegration is for the thousands of Taliban soldiers and village boys in our country who have been driven from their homes–either by fair means or intimidation, by bad behavior on the part of the NATO forces or by bad behavior by Afghan forces–and who do not stand ideologically against the Afghan people or the international community. They must be persuaded by all means to return."[24]

The IC quickly agreed to support this initiative. The Afghan conceived, Afghan led, and Afghan executed program is supported by the UNDP serving as the trustee. The APRP trust fund pays for the daily operations of the Joint Secretariat (JS) in Kabul and of the Provincial Joint Secretariat Teams (PJST) in each province, as well as outreach events to inform the various audiences on the APRP, demobilization of former fighters, and community recovery projects and programs. As an example, funding for 2012 was US$173.5 million. Although this is an Afghan owned process, support of the IC including ISAF and the U.S. has been necessary from the beginning. Within ISAF HQ, the Forces Reintegration Cell (FRIC) has been established not only to incorporate the reintegration and reconciliation in staff work but also to cooperate with the JS; in addition, the U.S. military established the Afghan Hands program that has provided administrative capacities to the PJST. Within the Regional

---

[23] See annex 1. The development of the APRP is described in HQ ISAF, Force Reintegration Cell, *A Guide to the Afghan Peace and Reintegration Program (APRP)*, March 2012, Kabul, 4-6. Available at:
https://ronna.apan.org/FRIC/APRP%20Policy%20Documents%20Structures%20and%20SOPs/Reintegration_Hand_Book.pdf (accessed February 14, 2014).
[24] Susanne Koebl and Ralf Neukirch, "Spiegel Interview with Hamid Karzai: 'There has to be Peace now'," *Der Spiegel*, English Language Edition (January 31, 2010) (http://www.spiegel.de/international/world/0,1518,6751400,00.html) (accessed December 28, 2013).

Commands, staff elements are incorporated that deal with the military support of reintegration.

Four years later, reintegration numbers indicate that the APRP has been surprisingly successful. As of 2013, it has enabled more than 7,300 insurgent fighters to renounce violence and rejoin society, while recidivism rates have remained extremely low.[25] Considering these significant accomplishments leads to this question: how does the APRP differ from previous, less successful DDR programs[26] that were executed in Afghanistan from 2003 to 2007, and how does the APRP factor in the lessons from DDR in other countries?

3.1 Preceding Programs from 2003 until 2007

The Afghan New Beginnings Program began in October 2003 and ended in July 2005.[27] Its objectives were to disarm and demobilize

---

[25] Numbers are available at the UNDP webpage:

http://www.af.undp.org/content/afghanistan/en/home/operations/projects/crisi s_prevention_and_recovery/aprp/ (accessed February 14, 2014). See also the numbers provided by Major General Hook in Cheryl Pellerin, "Afghan Insurgent Reintegration Effort Works," *U.S. Department of Defense Information*, February 22, 2012. Next to reintegration within the APRP, 'silent reintegration' occurs. Numbers or estimates on 'silent reintegration' are not available. See also Alexander, "Decomposing an Insurgency," 50. Although not part of the APRP, reintegration also comprises returning refugees. See Alpaslan Oezerdem, Abdul Hai Sofizada, "Sustainable reintegration to returning refugees in post-Taliban Afghanistan: land-related challenges," *Conflict, Security & Development*, 6:1, April 2006, 75-100.

[26] The assessment that the previous DDR processes did not work is shared, among others, by Steven A. Zyk, "Former combatant reintegration and fragmentation in contemporary Afghanistan", *Conflict, Security & Development*, 9:1, April 2009, 111; Paula Hanasz, "Appeasing 'upset brothers': an introduction to the Afghanistan Peace and Reintegration Program," *Australian Journal of International Affairs*, vol. 66, no. 2, April 2012, 155-168. See also Max Boot, *Invisible Armies. An Epic History of Guerrilla Warfare from Ancient Times to the Present,* (New York/London: Liveright Publishing Corporation, 2013), XXIII.

[27] A short overview of the history of reintegration efforts in Afghanistan is provided by Amato, Jonathan N., "Tribes, Pashtunwali and how they impact reconciliation and reintegration efforts in Afghanistan," *Thesis submitted to the Faculty of the Graduate School of Arts and Sciences of Georgetown University in partial fulfillment of the requirements for the degree of Master of Arts in Security Studies,* Washington D.C., April 16, 2010, 26-30; Hanasz, "Appeasing 'upset brothers'," 158-159. The Afghan New

the Afghan Military Forces (AMF–the so called Northern Alliance)[28] as well as illegally armed groups. It was clear from the beginning that the buildup of a new Afghan state and society was intended to end the dominant role of armed parties and individual commanders.[29]

In spite of the positive effects on security brought about by the demobilization of more than 60,000 former fighters,[30] the primary aim was not achieved: DDR did not break the ties between the Afghan warlords and their militiamen, and it tackled only the AMF, not the illegally armed groups. In addition to these shortfalls, it became evident that vocational training of former soldiers corresponded with economic development as well as with development projects for the communities. The International Crisis Group had previously requested in 2003 to "identify and support the creation of sustainable economic opportunities for demobilized combatants as part of long-term regional development strategies that cover, inter alia, rehabilitation and development of Afghan industries, mining, forest management, and cotton production."[31]

Learning from the mistakes of the Afghan New Beginnings Program, the Afghan government introduced a new program called Disbandment of Illegal Armed Groups (DIAG) in late 2005. "Dis-

---

Beginnings Program was launched under the lead of UNAMA, with UNDP in responsibility for its execution.

[28] Afghan Militia Force (AMF). For more information, see the webpage of Global Security, http://www.globalsecurity.org/military/world/afghanistan/amf.htm (accessed January 3, 2014).

[29] International Crisis Group, *Disarmament and Reintegration in Afghanistan,* ICG Asia Report, no. 65, September 30, 2003, i. This report of the International Crisis Group is available on its webpage http://www.crisisgroup.org/en/regions/asia/south-asia/afghanistan/065-disarmament-and-reintegration-in-afghanistan.aspx. (accessed January 3, 2014).

[30] DDR led to the demobilization of 62.376 AMF members and the collection of 57,629 weapons. By the end of the reintegration phase, 88 percent of demobilized soldiers had received benefits in the form of agricultural, small business, and other vocational training. See *Small Arms Survey 2009*: Chapter 9, Summary "DDR in Afghanistan: When State-building and Insecurity Collide." (available at http://www.smallarmssurvey.org/fileadmin/docs/A-Yearbook/2009/en/Small-Arms-Survey-2009-Chapter-09-summary-EN.pdf) (accessed November 11, 2013).

[31] *Disarmament and Reintegration in Afghanistan ICG Asia Report N°65*, September 30, 2003, iii.

armament and law enforcement mechanisms are used to weaken commander–militiamen linkages, with special emphasis on breaking ties between elected government officials and their associated militias. Whereas DDR provided individual benefits, DIAG uses community development projects as incentives." DIAG also included the "threat of forcible compliance".[32]

This initiative was in line with the overall assessment of the Afghan government that the private militias of the warlords posed a greater threat to them than the Taliban insurgency.[33] But when the Taliban offensives began in 2008, DIAG became undermined. Warlords decided to keep their militias as a means of hedging against the potential return of the Taliban.[34] It was widely perceived that the ISAF forces were incapable of managing the Taliban threat alone.[35] In this respect, the comment of a governor in North Afghanistan is enlightening, as described by U.S. staff officer Christian M. Karsner and analyst Sarah E. Kopczynski assigned to Regional Command North (RC-N) in Masar-e-Sharif: "The governor told RC-N that because the insurgents use the larger weapons to threaten villagers, he would not take comparable weapons away from the villagers and send them home to be slaughtered for supporting the GIRoA (Government of the Islamic Republic of Afghanistan; U.H.) peace proc-

---

[32] "DIAG includes the threat of forcible compliance, though it has rarely been applied, if ever" (*Small Arms Survey 2009, 2*). The report underlines the correlation between disarmament and the credible threat of use of force.

[33] Vishal Chandra, "The Evolving Politics of Taliban. Reintegration and Reconciliation in Afghanistan," *Strategic Analysis*, vol. 35, no. 5, September 2011, 840.

[34] Christian M. Karsner, Sarah E. Kopczynski, "Through and with: Reintegration in Northern Afghanistan," *Special Warfare*, vol. 25, no.1 (Jan-Mar 2012), 7.

[35] "The coalition and the DIAG program were philosophically opposed to recognizing warlord militias. Hence, no attempt was made to convince extant warlords to mobilize their militias. Instead, other initiatives were tried, such as the Auxiliary Police (ANAP) program (2006 to 30 September 2008, which failed), the Afghan Public Protection Program (APPP), the Local Defense Initiative (2009) which was justified as traditional tribal defense forces called *Arbaki*, and finally the Afghan Local Police initiative, which succeeded the APPP in 2010. Additionally, the Coalition began a rapid build-up of the ANA beginning in late 2008. The problem was these programs required time, money, and resources." (Raymond Millen, *Personal Notes on Afghanistan*, 9).

ess."[36] Consequently, it became more important to redirect reintegration efforts against the new threat: the reemerging Taliban.

The Afghan DDR experience prior to the launch of the APRP mirrors several lessons learned from other theatres: both former combatants and their communities must benefit from incentives; reliable administrative bodies must be in place to run the procedures and provide support;[37] and the economy must enable former combatants to have a livelihood. Most importantly, security is a prerequisite for effective reintegration in the midst of a conflict. If, due to limited security, hedging behavior of warlords and village elders is prevalent, reintegration efforts will be undermined.

3.2   The Comprehensive Approach of the APRP

The APRP is the result of adapting DDR to a dynamic political and military environment. Due to its introduction in the midst of an insurgency, the program's reintegration efforts target those who fight the government, ignoring the militia forces, which lie in the shadows. They complement efforts to strengthen the state's security institutions as instruments to achieve compliance forcibly, if necessary. A suggested approach to APRP is as follows:

Afghan political Will to achieve Peace is clearly expressed

The APRP has long been politically supported by the Afghan state and society, as well as by the IC.[38] At the district and provincial level of government, thousands of tribal and community leaders agreed

---

[36] Karsner/Kopczynski, "Through and with: Reintegration in Northern Afghanistan," 7.

[37] The Afghan experience also stresses the need to check eligibility. Different groups of armed persons must be clearly separated to prevent that the same person takes part in different programs. In fact, many reintegrated militiamen were former AMF personnel.

[38] Nanasz, "Appeasing 'upset brothers'," 158. The IC's support is expressed by the APRP's budget that amounted to US$772 million over five years. The 'White Paper of the Interagency Policy Group's Report on U.S. Policy toward Afghanistan and Pakistan' released on 27 March 2009 pointed out the need for convincing non-ideologically committed insurgents to stop fighting and reintegrate, and that these efforts must be conducted by Afghans. See Annex 3.

upon the APRP at a consultative peace *Jirga* held in June 2010. As John Alexander underlines, "leadership by the provincial authorities has proved to be the key to success in implementing the APRP at local level."[39] In point of fact, buy-in of lower levels of government is given, although with different commitments. There are political reasons why some governors may not support reintegration since it would undermine patronage networks that serve as their power basis.

Next to authorities on provincial and district levels, the buy-in of the tribal leaders is a conditio-sine-qua-non, as the first Director FRIC, Major General Phil Jones, argues: "Reintegration is likely to be successful only when tribal and other local leaders are involved."[40]

However, a controversy exists as to what extent the tribes are important. Due to their fragmentation and erosion, Jonathan N. Amato argues, "The tribal system and Pashtunwali provide opportunities for reconciliation and reintegration, but could also pose obstacles to such efforts."[41] By contrast, the role of the mullahs and shurahs has increased. Reasons for the damage of the tribal system are related to the Soviet occupation, in which one million Pashtuns were killed and three million Afghans were displaced to refugee camps in Pakistan, where they were exposed to political influence that emphasized a more Islamist identity as opposed to a Pashtun nationalism. Nonetheless, even the religious indoctrination was heavily influenced by the Pashtunwali. Therefore, Amato concludes: "The end result was a group of detribalized warriors who, much as they might have claimed to fight solely for Islam, still carried with them many of the social attitudes, beliefs, and customs of the Pashtuns."[42] Finally, one may agree that the tribal culture remains important but has suffered from disruption in certain cases.

Another important issue that limits the support of the people is the hedging behaviour. The buy-in of local leaders may remain limited, so long as they perceive a need to hedge their communities

---

[39] Alexander, "Decomposing an Insurgency", 50. See also Jones, "Reintegrating Afghan Insurgents," 13.

[40] Jones, "Reintegrating Afghan Insurgents," 17.

[41] Amato, "Tribes, Pashtunwali and how they impact reconciliation and reintegration efforts in Afghanistan," 3.

[42] *Ibid.*, 15-18. See also Hanasz, "Appeasing 'upset brothers'," 158.

against insurgent groups that dominate their area. Since "population control" is an important objective of the insurgency, it can be assumed that insurgent groups place great emphasis on monitoring and sanctioning the local population. Thus, hedging behaviour explains why one son of a family or one young man living in a village may be an insurgent while at the same time another son or young man serves with the Afghan security forces.

In spite of the challenges mentioned above, the Afghan people were duly informed and their engagement sought, as the opinion polls of the Asia Foundation indicate.[43] The vast majority of the Afghans not only knew about the APRP but also had been very supportive of its political objectives.

In the end, one may state that the APRP is an Afghan owned process that seeks the active participation of the entire populace.[44] It also underscores the fact that the Afghan state and its people did not surrender to the insurgents; at the same time, however, neither the state nor the people are seeking a military solution and a decisive defeat of the insurgents but rather a sustainable peace, to which the former insurgents should contribute.

Peace through Grievance Resolution on all Levels

Within the framework of the APRP, the Afghan government established the High Peace Council (HPC).[45] The HPC addresses grievances that enflame insurgents to fight, and it brokers agreements

---

[43] The people's support is researched in the yearly opinion polls conducted by the Asia Foundation. See the survey of the Asia Foundation, *Afghanistan in 2012: A survey of the Afghan People 2012*, 53-62. Available at the webpage of the Asia Foundation, (http://asiafoundation.org/publications/pdf/1163; assessed December 29, 2013).

[44] Jones, "Reintegrating Afghan Insurgents," 11. The need for national ownership is stressed in United Nations Inter-agency Working Group on Disarmament, Demobilization and Reintegration, *Operational Guide to the Integrated Disarmament, Demobilization and Reintegration Standards*, 29.

[45] Background information is available at the ISAF webpage, www.isaf.nato.int/article/focus/afghanistan-peace-and-reconcialitation-program.html. (accessed February 14, 2014).

with insurgents.[46] Its main task is to lead the reconciliation efforts with the highest Taliban leadership.[47] At the provincial and district levels the HPC contributes to grievance resolution.[48] As Major General Hook, the second Director FRIC, explains: "A cornerstone of this local approach is the resolution of grievances that led people to fight in the first place. If you accept the premise that 80 percent of the men fighting in the south (of Afghanistan; U.H.) are fighting for nonideological reasons–and our analysis of why they have stopped fighting supports this–it becomes clear that if you can address their grievances, you can draw them back into society."[49] Thus, the insurgents' motivations to fight, which vary between the political level of the insurgents' leadership and their local groups, can be addressed more specifically.

The APRP is aligned with Afghan Culture

The APRP focuses on conflict resolution as an informal legal framework in accordance with Afghan traditions and reflects the nascent reality of the Afghan law enforcement and judicial system.[50] It takes advantage of the co-existence of newly established state authorities, such as the provincial and district governors, along with the traditional tribal system that places responsibilities on the village elders. All, but in particular the village elders, share responsibility for the success of the reintegration process.[51]

In Pashtun areas, Pashtunwali, the ethical code that determines daily life, is principally in harmony with reintegration, since this "customary law primarily seeks compensation based on social

---

[46] Karsner/Kopczynski, "Through and with: Reintegration in Northern Afghanistan," 35-43.

[47] See chapter 3.4

[48] Alexander, "Decomposing an Insurgency," 50.

[49] Major General Hook in Karen Parrish, "General: Afghan Reintegration Program will take time," *U.S. Department of Defense Information*, December 8, 2011.

[50] However, insurgents remain subject to prosecution in cases of significant human rights violations or major war crimes. See Parrish, Karen, "General: Afghan Reintegration Program will take time," *U.S. Department of Defense Information*, December 8, 2011.

[51] Karsner/Kopczynski, "Through and with: Reintegration in Northern Afghanistan," 6.

reconciliation."[52] Traditional culture, more than financial incentives, has inclined elders and village residents to receive former insurgents, to integrate them, and to take care that they do not defect. As Major General Hook underlines, "The individual has been accepted back and been forgiven, so he now is responsible for his behavior to the community."[53] If one feels honor-bound to continue his fight against the Afghan government and ISAF, he can be offered an honorable way out. An effective example of such an alternative, compensation payment for people killed by U.S./ISAF personnel plays an important role in preventing attacks as a response requested by honour.

In addition, the Afghan culture of warfare also plays a supportive role in the reintegration effort. Traditionally, Afghans do not engage in unlimited wars. Often, their goal is simply to draw a better bargain with greater benefits.[54] Consequently, switching sides in wars has become an accepted habit that facilitates reintegration progress. As analyst Seth G. Jones concludes: "Over the past several decades of warfare in Afghanistan, low-, mid-, and even senior-level fighters have regularly changed sides. Indeed, reintegration is an integral part of Afghan culture."[55] However, one must acknowledge that each village or insurgent group may differ in its cultural suitability for reintegration.[56]

Targets are former Combatants and Communities

While former combatants benefit from transitional payments, the communities who receive these persons are awarded with development projects. A tier 1 project can be up to $25.000; Community Development Committees (CDC) can nominate any number of Tier 1 projects totalling no more than $50.000. Tier 2 projects can be up to $200.000 and are nominated by District Development Assemblies

---

[52] Jones, "Reintegrating Afghan Insurgents," 17.

[53] Major General Hook cited in Pellerin, Cheryl, "Afghan Insurgent Reintegration Effort Works," *U.S. Department of Defense Information*, February 22, 2012.

[54] Suicide and insider attacks are apparently not part of this culture. They are a new form of warfare in the Afghan theatre.

[55] Jones, "Reintegrating Afghan Insurgents," 1.

[56] Amato, "Tribes, Pashtunwali and how they impact reconciliation and reintegration efforts in Afghanistan," 40.

(DDA). Each DDA can nominate up to two Tier 2 small grant projects. The development of the proposals is placed in the hands of the communities to ensure that they match their needs and gain their commitment. The substantial funds available for community projects underline that "the community rather than the insurgent is rewarded for accepting the insurgent back".[57]

However, a dilemma exists that has been appearing in several stability operations, such as in the Balkans during the NATO intervention: often, development support is given to provinces, districts, or communities being assessed as highly insecure, while peaceful communities remain neglected. Thus, non-compliant behaviour is "rewarded". APRP suffers from this dilemma as well; consequently, the development portion of the APRP must be closely coordinated with the development aid delivered by development agencies in the framework of the whole-of-government approach,[58] and also with IOs and NGOs.

Central Responsibility but local Execution

Within the Afghan government bureaucracy, the Joint Secretariat (JS), an independent ministry, oversees the program. All applications for reintegration as well as all proposals for community projects are forwarded to the JS for approval and provision of funding. However, the responsibility for the execution lies with the Provincial Joint Secretariat Teams (PJST) that possess the authority to run the assigned programs (outreach, demobilization, community development). They interact with all stakeholders, execute the various education and training courses, and closely track the former combatants.

The APRP operates within the government administrative structures, thus serving as a catalyst for further improving the state's capacities and capabilities. Thus, the program contributes to what US-sociologist Charles Tilly labeled as "state making through war making".[59]

---

[57] Johnson, "Reintegration and Reconciliation in Afghanistan," 98.
[58] See here chapter 7.
[59] Charles Tilly, „How War Made States and Vice Versa," *Center for Studies of Social Change, New School for Social Research*, 1987.

It is no surprise that significant bureaucratic challenges hamper the execution of the APRP. They are mainly caused by the inefficiency of nascent state structures.[60] Here, another dilemma exists: Afghan ownership has been helpful in establishing the general acceptance of the APRP among insurgents and the people. Nonetheless, due to insufficient capacities and capabilities, many significant problems have emerged, notably the haphazard distribution of budget funding.

In 2012, payments for former combatants as well as for community projects were delayed for many months. So far, former combatants as well as community members have shown surprising patience. In spite of the delayed flow of funds, the communities continued to press forward with an increasing number of project proposals throughout 2012 and 2013.

These shortfalls can partly be attributed to strict regulations of the UNDP implemented to counter corruption. However, as Karsner and Kopczynski underscore, the biggest challenge is the "over-centralization of decision-making at the Kabul level and insufficient involvement of communities and districts, which thwarts a bottom-up approach." They warned in 2011: "If the GIRoA appears weak, corrupt or insincere in the eyes of the Afghan people and the insurgents and continues to thwart bottom-up solutions, the early success of reintegration will not continue."[61]

Unfulfilled promises may place the entire program at risk.[62] These risks must be balanced with the positive impact of APRP on state building. Improving administrative processes over time helps build state structures beyond the capital of Kabul and, as a consequence, increases the legitimacy of the central government. Among the diverse challenges the Afghan government has been facing, overcoming the still existing lack of legitimacy is of utmost importance.

---

[60] The danger of creating hollow state structures during stability operations is analyzed by Berit Bliesemann de Guevara, Florian P. Kühn, *Illusion Statebuilding. Warum sich der westliche Staat so schwer exportieren lässt*, Hamburg (Koerber Stiftung), 2010.

[61] Karsner/Kopczynski, "Through and with: Reintegration in Northern Afghanistan," 11.

[62] Jones, "Reintegrating Afghan Insurgents," 16.

As scholar Raymond Millen argues, "the long-term threat to Afghanistan is not the Taliban but structural imbalances in power".[63]

A major strategic deficit exists that is not easy to fix. What is Pakistan's role in fuelling the insurgency in Afghanistan? Was APRP coordinated with Pakistan's government? It is apparent that this country has had a strategic interest in supporting the Taliban.[64] Nonetheless, since the Taliban threatened its government and its people, the Pakistani armed forces have conducted offensive operations in its western provinces, in particular in the Federal Administered Tribal Areas (FATA). These forces have included reintegration in their operational design. However, their approach was different from the APRP. Building schools and conducting vocational training, they pursued rather the traditional CIMIC approach that aims at contributing to force protection.

Overall, the APRP has generated surprisingly positive results with strategic effects. Still, the program possesses an extremely high potential that has yet to be reached: it is a comprehensive program that improves security, increases the government administrative capacity and capabilities and thus its legitimacy; it enhances development (meeting the needs of the people in the short term), and empowers the people not only through education and vocational training but also through their methods of achieving conflict resolutions and peace settlements.

3.2   Reintegration in the Midst of a Conflict

What are the reasons that APRP has been quite successful in spite of the ongoing fighting, administrative shortfalls and the countermeasures of the insurgents' leadership? One reason is that security preceded reintegration.[65] The differences in security and reintegration numbers among the regions in Afghanistan support this assertion. Regional Command (RC) North and RC West are assessed as more

---

[63] Raymond A. Millen, "Time for a Strategic and Intellectual Pause in Afghanistan," *Parameters*, Summer 2010, 36.

[64] Robert M. Gates, *Duty. Memoirs of a Secretary at War*, New York (Alfred A. Knopf) 2014, 371-372. See also Ahmed Rashid, *Descent into Chaos*, New York (Penguin) 2008.

[65] See Jones, "Reintegrating Afghan Insurgents," IX.

secure than the other RCs. Here, a lower number of critical incidents, such as ambushes, IED attacks, insider and suicide attacks, occur. Consequently, the numbers of reintegrated former combatants are significantly higher.[66]

In general, security and its perceived improvement are important facilitators of re-integration.[67] The importance of the perception of security on a local level is expressed by Linda Robinson in her book about the buildup of the Afghan Local Police (ALP). She argues: "In a place as intimidated as Paktika, villagers were not going to come forward unless they were convinced the new leaders stood a chance of winning."[68] Due to the withdrawal of ISAF/U.S. combat forces, these fighting credentials must be established by the ANSF. Chief among these is fighting in such a way that collateral damage is prevented to the greatest extent possible. This puts emphasis on incorporating collateral damage avoidance into the ANSF and, consequently, into the training of the ANSF by ISAF Security Forces Assistance (SFA) teams.

Based on their experience in North Afghanistan, Karsner and Kopczynski stress the need to continue military operations and to put pressure on the insurgents: "Success in RC-North demonstrated that persistent pressure from lethal operations and kill-capture missions that targeted insurgent leaders were highly effective in undermining insurgent confidence and establishing a strategic advantage. Interviews with candidates for reintegration revealed that missions to remove insurgent leaders significantly pressured successive leaders and their subordinate fighters to consider reintegration for fear of being next on the target list."[69] However, extreme care must be taken: killed or captured leaders are usually quickly replaced by younger, less experienced, but often more radical leaders; in areas

---

[66] Karsner/Kopczynski, "Through and with: Reintegration in Northern Afghanistan," 11. They argue that the better security situation in the North allowed a RC North-wide implementation of the program.

[67] *Ibid.*, 4. See also Bob Woodward, *Obama's Wars*, New York/ London/Toronto/Sydney (Simon&Schuster): 2010, 220.

[68] Linda Robinson, *One Hundred Victories. Special Ops and the Future of American Warfare*, New York (Public Affairs): 2013, 79.

[69] Karsner/Kopczynski, "Through and with: Reintegration in Northern Afghanistan," 3.

where Special Forces conduct raids, a point of no return may be reached where reintegration efforts are strongly rejected by the fighters but also by the local populace.[70]

Nevertheless, it is highly justifiable to argue that the U.S. surge,[71] together with the buildup of the ALP, has decisively contributed to the integration progress. But this correlation between security and reintegration is not so apparent at the local level. Reintegration also occurs in districts and communities that are highly contested.

A more complex approach to analyzing reintegration successes may be the examination of insurgent motivations. Most of the insurgents in Afghanistan are not spurred on by ideology. In general, 80 percent do not fight out of this motivation. David Kilcullen underpins that most insurgents are "accidental guerilla". Consequently, the U.S. and NATO are wrong if they assess all of insurgents as members of a terrorist network.[72]

Motivations can be categorized as follows:

1)   Intimidation or coercion (including economic needs);
2)   Religious motivation or ideology;
3)   The perception of the government as illegitimate and corrupt or the lack of governance; and
4)   Hatred of foreign forces.

The reasons, which apply may vary from region to region, and even from village to village.

Intimidation or coercion is mainly an issue of security. If village elders perceive the security situation to be such that the insurgents' intimidation demands hedging behavior, they may, at the same time, support insurgent groups as well as the ANSF by sending

---

[70] See the COIN mathematics in chapter 3.5.

[71] The strategic discussions on the U.S. surge in 2009 are reflected in Woodward, *Obama's Wars*.

[72] Kilcullen, David, *The Accidental Guerrilla. Fighting small wars in the midst of a big one*, (Oxford: University Press 2009), 30-114. Consequently, the recourse to the question why insurgents fight against the Afghan government and ISAF is helpful to better understand the strategic environment as well as the potential progress of reintegration. See also Joes, Anthony James, *Resisting Rebellion. The History and Politics of Counterinsurgency*, (Lexington: University Press of Kentucky 2006), 166-168.

young men as reinforcements. In addition, economic deprivation may coerce young men to fight

Coerced insurgents often do not fight for religious reasons, at least not in the beginning. For the insurgents' commanders, by contrast, religion is a tool to motivate insurgents to fight. At the same time, religious arguments on the incompatibility of Quran and fighting the Afghan legal authorities may aid in motivating former insurgents to consider reintegration. Therefore, religious lessons designed to teach a moderate understanding of the Quran are an essential part of the demobilization programs.[73]

Coercion by terrorists can be overcome, particularly if the Afghan government's promise of a better, more secure future is shown to be credible in such governing and societal aspects as deployment of garrisoned or permanently available forces,[74] the presence of government officials, the completion of relevant development projects, and economic opportunities. The decision to reintegrate (if made by elders or the insurgent himself) is a life changing

---

[73] Amato sees opportunities to utilize religion for peace and stability, but for the Afghan government rather than for ISAF or the U.S. See Amato, "Tribes, Pashtunwali and how they impact reconciliation and reintegration efforts in Afghanistan," 41.

[74] In this respect, the creation and deployment of the Afghan Local Police (ALP) is providing better local security as well as job opportunities. The strategic background of establishing the ALP and its implementation is described by Robinson, *One Hundred Victories; s*ee also Fred Kaplan, *The Insurgents. David Petraeus and the Plot to change the American Way of War*, (New York/London/Toronto/Sydney/ New Delhi: Simon&Schuster, 2013), 341. Raymond Millen points out: "In practice, conventional forces generally exhaust themselves conducting iterative clearing operations (e.g. counterguerrilla) and raids, which have no lasting effect. If insurgents retain the means to enter a 'cleared' area again, then counterguerrilla warfare is not decisive and hence remains a suboptimal solution." (Raymond A. Millen, "Time for a Strategic and Intellectual Pause in Afghanistan", *Parameters*, Summer 2010, 37). Steven Metz underlines the risks involved with the buildup of local security forces, based on the Iraq case. "They are a true Pandora's box, hard to close where once opened." (Steven Metz, *Iraq & the Evolution of American Strategy*, (Washington D.C.: Potomac Books, 2008), 189). Based on experience in African conflicts, retired Colonel and military professor Prosper Zena emphasizes the transition of former combatants into civilian life, not the security services. He advises, "Governments should be intensely circumspect when considering the viability of militants and ex-combatants as potential security providers." (Zena, "The Lessons and Limits of DDR in Africa," 8).

moment. The individual must be sure of gaining the best outcome in his cost-benefit-analysis. In the end, the benefit of changing sides to the Afghan government must lie in the fulfilment of the individual's desire for better security and services.

The existence of grievances without resolution by the Afghan authorities and the perception of the Afghan government as corrupt and illegitimate may also inspire men to join the insurgency. This seems to be a major factor, as Seth G. Jones points out, based on the sample of 36 reintegration cases: "… in 71 percent of the cases, insurgents reintegrated because of grievances."[75] In these cases, coercion by insurgents is not necessary. Re-integration can only be increased, in such circumstances, by improved grievance resolution delivered by state or state sponsored agents and good governance. Seeking a military solution to these kinds of socio-political problems is a recipe for never-ending conflict.

Hatred of foreign forces is another factor that fuels the conflict. This factor is more relevant in the South and East than in the West and North of Afghanistan. With the withdrawal of ISAF forces, this inclination may become less significant.

Considering its positive aspects, it is reasonable to conclude that the APRP has profited from DDR experiences elsewhere. It offers impressive insights as to how a state with the support of the IC can adapt DDR to meet changes most effectively in the country's political, cultural and economic environment. However, the new approach does carry risks by relying on the swift development of state structures and of the economy. As a result, its execution relies on a variety of disparate factors, requiring not only a long-term international financial commitment by the IC, but also the consistent political will, the continuous improvement of administrative capacities and capabilities, apolitical support provided by the security institutions (i.e., military, police, intelligence services), and the enduring commitment of the people to live together with former adversaries and potentially dissatisfied former combatants.

The main difference from previous DDR programs is the APRP's reintegration effort in the midst of a conflict. It becomes paramount, therefore, to consider the impact of ongoing war on rein-

---

[75] Jones, "Reintegrating Afghan Insurgents," IX.

tegration, from all aspects. First, due to the nature of war, the leaders of the various insurgent groups react to reintegration successes, often with increased indoctrination and harsh punishments of the families of insurgents who apply for reintegration. Second, the analysis of reintegration progress underlines the correlation between reintegration success and the (perceived) improved security situation. The insurgents' and people's perception that the Afghan government will persevere in the conflict benefits reintegration. Additionally, people who take advantage of effective reintegration programs are likely to perceive the Afghan government as superior. Third, the progress achieved so far may also be the result of strategic coordination of the APRP with President Barack Obama's decision on a military and civilian surge, in conjunction with the announced withdrawal of combat forces and the IC's continued commitment after their withdrawal. Nearly all of the major force contributing nations stated in 2011 and 2012 that they would continue their support for Afghanistan beyond 2014. Finally, the new policies of the government of Pakistan against the Taliban in its western provinces may have also contributed to the APRP progress. In the end, the APRP challenges the traditional approach of launching reintegration when peace is settled or at the final stage of war.[76] Reintegration programs indeed can be successfully developed and executed in the midst of a fierce conflict.

One may also deduce that ethnicity plays a major role in the decision to join the insurgency. In fact, the insurgency is mainly driven by the Pashtun population. However, the argument that the insurgency can only attract Pashtuns has been falsified by the developments that have arisen in Northern Afghanistan since 2008. Pashtun-led insurgency groups have been able to recruit significant numbers of Uzbek and a smaller number of Tajiks in areas outside the Pashtun pockets. The main reason for this successful recruitment was the policy of appointing Uzbeks and Tajks as local commanders and shadow governors. Helpful also in overcoming ethnic tensions has been the support of the clergy. Evidently, it is only to a limited extent that ethnicity matters as leverage in creating and maintaining the insurgency; tensions can be overcome by participation in power

---

[76] See Joes, *Resisting Rebellion,* 169.

and by references to the common bond of a shared religion. There-fore, one may logically conclude that ethnic groups do not exclude themselves either from fighting, or from reintegration.

In executing reintegration within the APRP, Afghanistan and the IC stressed that, while the time was not ripe for negotiations[77], peace and not an unconditional surrender of the various insurgent groups has become the overall political objective. In addition, the comprehensive grievance resolution approach has contributed to the reintegration progress, and the announced withdrawal of ISAF may play out positively as long as the Afghan National Security Forces (ANSF) are strong enough and perceived as such by the people.

3.4. Reintegration and Reconciliation

Both, reconciliation and reintegration are integral elements of the APRP. Working simultaneously, they differ in the audiences they target. While reintegration aims to reinsert non-ideologically driven low and mid-level commanders and their followers into communi-ties, reconciliation is directed towards the top Afghan insurgent lead-ership and their future role in Afghanistan. Consequently, both ele-ments of the APRP have different organizational structures and pro-cedures.[78] While reintegration is a formalized way of integrating those combatants who wish to end fighting, reconciliation is rather a nego-tiation process without any prescribed outcome.

Expected to reinforce each other, reintegration and recon-ciliation are designed as complementary programs.[79] However, does that mean that the "success and failure of one rests largely (though not exclusively) with the success or failure of the other"?[80]

---

[77] Negotiations were only envisioned with the political leadership of the insurgency in the framework of the reconciliation process. See Johnson, "Reintegration and Reconciliation in Afghanistan," 97-101; Hanasz, "Appeasing 'upset brothers': an introduction to the Afghanistan Peace and Reintegration Program," 158.

[78] On Kabul level, a 70-member High Peace Council (HPC) under the leadership of the former president Burhanuddin Rabbani was established. On provincial level, Provincial Peace Councils (PPC) were created to cover the regional and local pecu-liarities.

[79] Hanasz, "Appeasing 'upset brothers': an introduction to the Afghanistan Peace and Reintegration Program", 156.

[80] *Ibid.*, 158.

The APRP was launched in 2010, in parallel not only with the U.S. surge, but also with the announcement that the U.S. and ISAF combat forces would start their withdrawal from Afghanistan in 2011. The new operational design of the coalition forces, based on a mixture of short term COIN, Counter Terrorism and Security Forces Assistance (SFA), reflects the changes in the political objectives of the U.S. and the other troop contributing nations. The original intent to establish a democratic state was replaced by the political objective of leaving Afghanistan in a state of "good enough". It was sufficient to establish it as a country stabilized by an internal balance of power, capable of fighting the insurgency with its own means, and in which the Al Qaeda network was disrupted.

In spite of the overall support of the entire APRP, U.S. diplomats formulated clear preconditions for any peace arrangements with the Taliban leadership. In early 2010, Richard Holbrooke, the then U.S. envoy to Afghanistan and Pakistan, put it bluntly: "The United States is not in direct contact with Taliban leadership. Why not? Because they aren't renouncing al Qaeda. We're not going to talk to people who are affiliated with al Qaeda."[81] This rigid policy caused friction, also on tactical levels. Field commanders, who had conducted successful peace negotiations with local Taliban groups, had to renounce already made agreements.[82] The rigid decline of negotiations was probably not aligned with the intent of President Obama. He himself had not only shown significant personal interest in reintegration and reconciliation during the strategy development

---

[81] Sara A. Carter, "Some Taliban leaders seek reintegration; Fleeing commanders leaving fighters, military officials says," *The Washington Times*, February 18, 2010. In spite of this public statement, Holbrooke believed that only reconciliation could make an end to the war in Afghanistan. The State Department launched a secret operation to negotiate via Saudi Arabia with members of the Quetta Taliban. See Woodward, *Obama's Wars*, 170, 240-241. In fact, in 2002, then Secretary of Defense, Ronald Rumsfeld, denied any opportunities to seek a political solution with the Taliban leadership. They were also not invited to the Bonn Conference in December 2001. At this time, the future president Karsai was much more inclined to offer special political arrangements, even an amnesty, for Taliban political leaders. Some observers regard the early denial of talks as a failure. See Chandra, "The Evolving Politics of Taliban. Reintegration and Reconciliation in Afghanistan", 840.

[82] See Chandra, "The Evolving Politics of Taliban. Reintegration and Reconciliation in Afghanistan", 842; Kaplan, *The Insurgents*, 335-337.

process in 2009 but also seemed to assess these as a necessary way to safeguard the successful termination of the war in Afghanistan.[83]

The Taliban leadership also showed little inclination to respond to the offered negotiations. Indeed, why should they have joined peace talks when motivation was lacking? At that time, they had already gained the military initiative. They lived relatively safely in the Western provinces of Pakistan. In addition, time was on their side. They merely had to wait for the withdrawal of foreign troops. However, peace negotiations also would have brought some advantages: drone attacks that were likely to inflict even more casualties on their side, would probably have been decreased during the negotiation process; and the invitation to peace talks would not have been merely a clear political signal that the Taliban were an important political power but also would have been an opportunity in which to include their interests in the shaping of Afghanistan's future.[84]

Today, in 2014, the situation is stalemated. No significant progress has been achieved so far. Only the positions of the stakeholders have changed. The U.S. appears more inclined to conduct peace talks with the Taliban[85]. The latter's willingness has also increased, since the withdrawal of foreign troops was a declared prerequisite for assuming peace talks. In fact, the Afghan government

---

[83] Reconciliation is not a new idea. Previously, the Soviets had developed the idea of reconciliation as part of stabilizing Afghanistan after their withdrawal in 1989. The Soviet reconciliation program is described in Peter Cooper, "The Soviet Experience in Afghanistan 1978-1989," in Helmut Hammerich, Uwe Hartmann, Claus von Rosen (ed.), *Jahrbuch Innere Führung 2010. Die Grenzen des Militärischen*, Berlin (Miles-Verlag) 2010, 174-201. This was taken up by the then Afghan President Najibullah, who intended reconciliation with the Islamists factions of the Peshawar group in early 1990 when the Soviet support came to an end. Later reconciliation efforts are described by Chandra, "The Evolving Politics of Taliban. Reintegration and Reconciliation in Afghanistan", 839-843. See also Larry Goodson, Thomas H. Johnson, "Parallels with the Past – How the Soviets Lost in Afghanistan, how the Americans are Losing," *Orbis*, Fall 2011, 580-582.

[84] The pros and cons are discussed in more detail by Stephen Biddle, "War Termination in Afghanistan," *Council on Foreign Relations*, October 29, 2013. Available at the webpage www.cfr.org/afghanistan/war-termination-afghanistan/p31742 (accessed May 29, 2014).

[85] Peace talks must also include Pakistan.

under President Karsai appeared less inclined to negotiations with the Taliban in spite of its public appeals.[86]

Coming back to the question raised earlier on the dependency on the success and failure of reintegration and reconciliation, one may argue that they can profit from each other. On the one side, reintegration and reconciliation support each other, at least at the local and regional levels. Concurrently, reintegration contributes to reinforcing the institution-building process of the Afghan state. Reconciliation will only be successful, however, if the state's institutions are strong enough to incorporate members of the insurgency leadership.

Reintegration progress will also foster the people's perception that reconciliation is the path to a more peaceful future. Opinion polls indicate that the Afghans are more optimistic and supportive of reintegration than of reconciliation.[87] This reflects their concern that

---

[86] The importance of a negotiation settlement after 2014 is underlined by Stephen Biddle, "War Termination in Afghanistan". Based on his assumption of a stalemated war in Afghanistan, he argues: "If the ANSF is not able to defeat the Taliban on the battlefield, this leaves only two plausible long term outcomes to the war. One would be a negotiated compromise settlement with the Taliban at some point, sooner or later. The other is defeat for the Afghan government via eventual defunding of the ANSF war effort. If defeat is to be avoided, then the purpose of the war is now to shape the terms of a future settlement to make them more favorable, and to make the settlement more sustainable once reached." He also raises the issue of the willingness of the U.S. Congress to accept compromise with the Taliban. If properly negotiated, Biddle argues, the settlement "could at least preserve the two vital U.S. national interests at stake in Afghanistan: that Afghan soil not become a base for militants to attack the West, and that it not become a base for destabilizing Afghanistan's neighbors." The reconciliation policies of the Afghan government are analyzed by Zeng Xiangyu, Zhang Chunyan, Zhu Yufan, "Political reconciliation in Afghanistan: Progress, challenges and prospects," *Strategic Studies*, Winter 2012/Spring 2013, 107-117. Available at the webpage: www.issi.org.pk/publication-files/1379480196_47959077.pdf) (accessed May 29, 2014). They are in line with Stephen Biddle's assessment when they conclude: "prospects for a political settlement of the Afghan conflict could be more promising if all sides understand that the present deadlock is by no means an accident and military means could hardly make big breakthrough." (114)

[87] Hanasz, "Appeasing 'upset brothers': an introduction to the Afghanistan Peace and Reintegration Program", 162; Asia Foundation, *Afghanistan in 2012. A Survey of the Afghan People*, 53-61. Available at:

reconciliation with the Taliban would negatively impact the quality of human rights and education achieved so far. On the other side, reconciliation progress may require limiting reintegration numbers in order not to erode further the supporting base for the insurgencies' leadership. In this case, politicians are likely to attempt to slow down the administrative execution of the reintegration processes. Political intervention may be one of the major reasons why the number of reintegrated former combatants is significantly lower in the East and South than in the other regions of Afghanistan. In the end, it is helpful to view reintegration and reconciliation as complementary. However, the progress achieved in the North and the West also underlines the fact that reintegration success is possible even without any progress in reconciliation with an opponents' leadership.[88]

Can reintegration and reconciliation be coordinated on a time table? Some arguments favor starting either with reconciliation *or* with reintegration. In the end, the answer to this question depends on the context. It is probably not reasonable to start with reconciliation in a conflict driven by ideology. In such a case, stalemates and interruptions are likely, and the entire process would probably take years before any agreements could be achieved.[89] There is no need to delay reintegration until reconciliation progress with the insurgencies' leadership is achieved. A pragmatic approach would be to start with reintegration and reconciliation simultaneously, as has been done in Afghanistan.

---

www.asiafoundation.org/resources/pdfs/surveybook2012web1.pdf   (accessed April 7, 2014). Since 2010, the data have showed increased support, in particular among the Pashtuns.

[88] The issue of reconciliation and the police is discussed in Samuel Musa, John Morgan, Matt Keegan, "Policing and COIN Operations. Lessons Learned, Strategies and Future Directions," *Center for Technology and National Security Policy. The Combating Terrorism Technical Support Office*, 2011.

[89] The Paris Peace Talks between the U.S. and Vietnam to end the Vietnam War between 1968 and 1973 may serve as an example of the potential duration of negotiations.

3.5 The Development of the U.S. Strategy in 2009 and the Significance of Reintegration

Reintegration (together with reconciliation) was an important element of consideration in the U.S. strategy making process that led to President Obama's decision on the employment of additional military forces and civilian resources (the 'surge') in Afghanistan in 2010.[90] Very early, he stated his support for the APRP publicly: "We will support efforts by the Afghan government to open the door to those Taliban who abandon violence and respect the human rights of their fellow citizens."[91]

During the strategic discussion group's meetings in 2009, Obama himself raised the issue of reintegration and reconciliation as overarching political initiatives. Apparently, the U.S. president saw progress in these fields as a precondition for the envisioned drawdown of the coalition's troops.[92] Thus, reintegration and reconciliation have become essential pillars of the new U.S. strategy.

The strategic discussions on Capitol Hill were triggered by the military's assessment that significant troop reinforcements were necessary to prevent losing the war in Afghanistan. General Stanley McChrystal and also his predecessor, General David D. McKiernan, stressed that the war would be lost if the troops were not reinforced significantly. The debate among the U.S. strategic leaders was questioning if a fully resourced COIN strategy was necessary and feasible, or if the strategy should focus exclusively on Counterterrorism (CT). Another issue raised was the question of whether the Taliban had to be defeated or whether their network alone had to be disrupted.[93] The strategy makers also struggled with even more fundamental topics: What was the right approach to Pakistan, an unstable Islamic country with nuclear weapons that supported the insurgency in Af-

---

[90] The discussion process is reconstructed in Woodward, *Obama's Wars*, and in Gates, *Duty*, 335-386.

[91] See Obama's speech at West Point in December 2009: "Full Transcript: President Obama's Speech on Afghanistan," *ABC News*, available at: http://abcnews.go.com/Politics/full-transcript-president-obamas-speech-afghanistan-delivered-west/story?id=9220661&page=2) (accessed October 10, 2013).

[92] Woodward, *Obama's Wars*, 229. See also Annex 2 of this book.

[93] Woodward, *Obama's Wars*, 113.

ghanistan due to its strategic calculus? They realized the limits of U.S. power in dealing with this "most dangerous country of the world", and they did not find leverage to prevent Pakistan from continuing its support for the Taliban.[94]

Often, the discussions among the strategic leaders and their advisors came back to defining the objectives of the Afghan war. The war had been ongoing for eight years at the time, but it was still not clear what the core objectives were.[95]

U.S. President Barack Obama did not want to support an open-ended commitment.[96] Afghanistan had been a limited war. He had to balance the war effort with issues of domestic and foreign policies, and also with the objectives and capabilities of allies and partners that were contributing to ISAF. He knew too well that the U.S. could not kill their way out of Afghanistan. He was familiar not only with the history of the Vietnam War but also with the fate of the Soviet military in Afghanistan: the Soviet armed forces at that time killed one million insurgents, and yet they had more opponents at the end of the conflict than at the beginning of the occupation. He was determined as well to avoid the mistake of waging a war that lacked a sound strategy.[97]

While Obama's military strategic leaders did not offer him additional strategic options besides the deployment of differently sized reinforcements to Afghanistan, it was the President himself and his personal staff who sought alternatives, or at least ways to mitigate the threat of again reinforcing a war with troops that cannot be won, as had happened in Vietnam. His intellectual approach was broader since he did not focus so much on military victory or defeat.

Obama's insistence on new approaches underlined the idea that he wanted to balance the military demands for a fully resourced people-centric COIN with other ways and means. He may have con-

---

[94] *Ibid.*, 89. See also Gates, *Duty*, 372.

[95] *Ibid.*, 185. Differences in defining the objectives had occurred previously at the beginning of the war. See Donald Rumsfeld, *Known and Unknown. A Memoir*, New York (Penguin Group) 2011, 398.

[96] Hew Strachan, *The Direction of War*, New York (Cambridge University Press) 2013, 228.

[97] Nick Lindley, "Redpointing Strategy: A Model for Strategy-making in Contemporary Conflict," *Royal College of Defence Studies*, July 2013, 17.

sidered that reintegration and reconciliation could serve as mitigating factors or even as objectives for the military. With respect to the importance of reintegration and reconciliation, he was supported by his Secretary of Defense, Robert Gates.[98] Nonetheless, neither of them managed to link the political objectives of the Afghan government as documented in the APRP with their own political objectives and the potential ways and means to achieve them.[99] Thus, the full potential of the APRP was not fully utilized in the U.S. strategy making process, meaning that friction would be sure to follow.

The senior military leaders did not appear to be resistant to the significance of reintegration. In contrast, supporting and enhancing the respective Afghan programs was one of the four elements of General McChrystal's new operational approach.[100] He saw reintegration as the "... logical outcome of a counter-insurgency campaign".[101]

General McChrystal argued that "killing an insurgent may make enemies of his father, sons, brothers and friends, whereas removing the cause for conflict does not."[102] If the killing of people increases the strength of the enemy, reintegration is a more suitable approach to fighting the insurgency. Consequently, killing the enemy was secondary to reintegration.[103]

At first glance, the political and the military views of reintegration fit together. Consequently, the result of the strategy development process was not only a decision made to increase the U.S.

---

[98] Gates, *Duty*, 366.

[99] Besides the Afghan government, NATO's relevance in the U.S. strategy making was very low. See Strachan, *The Direction of War*, 232.

[100] Woodward, *Obama's Wars*, 165. It was a strategic decision of President Obama to appoint General McChrystal as the new commander of ISAF to increase the utility of the U.S. surge. See the background information in Woodward, *Obama's Wars*, 83-85; Gates, *Duty*, 344-346.

[101] Alexander, ",Decomposing an Insurgency. Reintegration in Afghanistan," 48. See also Gates, *Duty*, 361.

[102] *Ibid.*, 50. See also Amato, who describes the automatic replacement of killed insurgents: "A younger man might be working while an older relative is off fighting, but will take up arms when the older relative is killed." (Amato, "Tribes, Pashtunwali and how they impact reconciliation and reintegration efforts in Afghanistan," 20).

[103] Woodward, *Obama's Wars*, 131

military and civilian forces but also to support the APRP politically and militarily. Considering these views and their result again, however, one can see that differences may, in fact, have existed, although they were not openly discussed. While General McChrystal saw reintegration as a means to support his operational-level COIN strategy, President Obama may have intended to utilize reintegration and reconciliation predominately at the political and strategic level as a way to prevent a second Vietnam.

Some interesting linkages between the new U.S. strategy for Afghanistan and the APRP can be constructed:

1), If the main objective is to defeat the insurgency and win militarily—as favored by then Secretary of Defense, Robert Gates, and his strategic advisors[104]—, reintegration loses relevance. Obama's final strategic guidance uses the term "to degrade the Taliban";[105] this gives more relevance to reintegration and other non-violent ways and means to fight the insurgency.

2), Since people are at the center of COIN, highest priority has to be placed on making people feel safer. Their protection must not be conducted by U.S. and ISAF forces alone. Consequently, the Afghan National Security Forces (ANSF) had to be built up faster, and the Afghan Local Police (ALP) had to stand up more rapidly in order to have holding forces available that could be deployed immediately after the successful completion of military operations. Improved security would have had a twofold effect: to convince combatants to reintegrate, and to foster the commitment of the people to socially integrating former insurgents.

3), The military reinforcements were deployed to "degrade the Taliban and set the conditions for accelerated transition to Afghan authorities". A major additional political objective was to prevent the perception of the U.S. as a weak superpower. The military and civilian surge also improved the conditions for reintegration pro-

---

[104] In the final order, "degrade Taliban" is the official wording. Secretary of Defense Robert Gates and his military advisors were in favor of "defeat". See Woodward, *Obama's Wars,* 386.

[105] "President Obama's final Orders for Afghanistan Pakistan Strategy, or terms sheet," in: Woodward, *Obama's Wars,* 385. The first paragraphs of the document are contained in Annex 2 of this book.

gress. Reintegration could be conducted from a position of strength, at the strategic as well as at the tactical level. This became an important prerequisite for the insurgent's decision to take advantage of the reintegration offer.

4), The surge of the U.S. and its allies and partners in 2010 can be seen through the lens of reintegration, thus offering a new perspective on the U.S. strategy making process under the leadership of President Obama. Reintegration was expected to support the surge's success by taking fighters from the battlefield and, thus, degrading the Taliban. It was the decisive way to prevent falling into the strategic trap of winning battles and, thus, losing the conflict.

Finally, one might argue that—from a strategic point of view that links political objectives with ways and means and that carefully analyzes the feasibility, acceptability, and suitability as well as the risks of its execution—the entire new U.S. strategy was designed to facilitate reintegration (and reconciliation). In this case, the surge was primarily aimed at improving the conditions for reintegration and reconciliation. Peace and conflict resolution through reintegration and reconciliation were the primary ends and ways. The surge of military and civil means was meant to set a framework, within which reintegration and reconciliation could thrive. It is not unlikely that President Obama assessed reintegration and reconciliation as strategies to decrease the likelihood of being even more drawn into the quagmire of a war without clearly defined objectives, and to maintain the U.S. international reputation in spite of the withdrawal of combat forces.

In this respect, it may be interesting to reflect upon the question of why the U.S. decided to announce a deadline publicly for the military withdrawal.[106] The main reasons were, in all probability, related to U.S. domestic politics; nonetheless, the decision may have also been made with an eye to the situation in Afghanistan. At the least, the early announcement of the military drawdown may have improved the conditions of reintegration and reconciliation. In addi-

---

[106] The implications of withdrawal from Afghanistan are discussed by Paul R. Kan, "Making a Sandwich in Afghanistan: How to Assess a Strategic Withdrawal from a Protracted Irregular War", *Small Wars Journal*, February 2011, 1-13. Available at http://smallwarsjournal.com/blog/journal/docs-temp/682-kan.pdf

tion to this possible benefit, the withdrawal of foreign forces from Afghan soil has not only been supportive in encouraging fighters to reintegrate (in particular those motivated by hatred of foreign troops) but also in facilitating reconciliation between the Afghan government and the insurgency top leaders who had requested the absence of foreign combat forces as a precondition for any peace talks.

On the other hand, as Paula Hanasz argues, the announced withdrawal and its deadline "weakens the GIRoA's bargaining position because it can not longer use it as a tangible outcome to offer insurgency leadership in return for its own demands."[107] However, from the U.S. position, the withdrawal of the coalition troops should never have become subject to negotiations conducted by the Afghan government with the Taliban or other insurgents' leadership.

In his guidance dated November 29, 2009, the U.S President recognized the importance of reintegration and reconciliation. He stressed both as "essential pillars of our strategy". Nonetheless, one might argue that the U.S. utilized reintegration as a means to pursue its national political interests (never again Vietnam, no loss of international reputation) and to execute the operational COIN strategy in order to prevent losing the war.

The political objectives that the Afghan government finally laid down in its APRP were not properly taken into account. There are good reasons for this neglect, notably, the pessimism that prevailed among the Afghan government as well as the IC when the APRP was launched in 2010. The Afghan communist regime under President Mohammed Nadschibullah (1986-1992) had not succeeded in its reconciliation efforts. From a conceptual point of view, reintegration was usually limited to post-conflict scenarios. Furthermore, the lessons learned from reintegration efforts during the Vietnam War also did not boost optimism.[108] Nonetheless, the U.S. new strat-

---

[107] Hanasz, "Appeasing 'upset brothers': an introduction to the Afghanistan Peace and Reintegration Program", 161.

[108] The U.S. implemented the Civil Operations and Revolutionary Development Support (CORDS) during the Vietnam War. See William P. Schoux, "The Vietnam CORDS Experience: A Model of successful civil-military Partnership?"; available at https://dec.usaid.gov/dec/content/Detail.aspx?q (accessed April 18, 2014); Dale Andrade, James H. Willbanks, CORDS/Phoenix, "Counterinsurgency Lessons from Vietnam for the Future," *Military Review*, March-April 2006, 9-23.

egy and the APRP reveal a disconnect: the strategic ends, ways and means of the Afghan and the U.S. governments were not aligned; and in its implementation, the U.S. armed forces attempted to disrupt, degrade and, possibly, defeat the insurgents through offensive military operations, reinforced by civilian efforts rather than by supporting the Afghan government's peace efforts.

4 Reintegration and Strategic Thought

This chapter examines the linkage between reintegration and strategic theory, addressing the following questions: Do theories of war and strategy enable us to better understand reintegration in the midst of a conflict? Do they even provide advice for the incorporation of reintegration in the development of strategies?[109]

4.1 Continuation of Politics and Policies

German strategic theorist Carl von Clausewitz's most relevant insight is the permanent dependence of war on policies and politics.[110] He realized this basic interdependence when he tested the ideal of absolute war against the historical reality of war. War does not necessarily escalate to its absolute form; rather, it often remains limited. This limitation is mainly due to the "intrinsically political nature of war," as Clausewitz biographer Raymond Aron summarized the theorist's main conclusion.[111]

Clausewitz argues that "war is simply a continuation of political intercourse, with the addition of other means. We deliberately use the phrase 'with the addition of other means' because we also want to make it clear that *war in itself does not suspend political intercourse or change it into something entirely different* (my emphasis). In essentials that intercourse continues, irrespective of the means it deploys. The

---

[109] The relationship between the theory and practice of war is described in Gray, *Modern Strategy*, 3. Gray refers to Bernard Brodie, who defined "… strategic theory (as) … a theory for action." (Bernhard Brodie, *War and Politics* (New York, 1973), 452. Gray argues that "theory and practice, as always, intertwine in the pragmatic world of strategy" (Gray, *On Strategy*, 273); see also his foreword in Metz, Steven, *Iraq & the Evolution of American Strategy*, (Washington D.C.: Potomac Books, 2008), VII-IX.

[110] In the language of the German original, Clausewitz uses the term "Politik". "Politik" is twofold: It means the policy of the state's government; however, it also comprises the entire interplay of all stakeholders including the different institutions of the national or international security system. Consequently, all actors of state and society on all sides of the belligerents and, indeed, of the neutral states have to be assessed by their impact on a war.

[111] Aron, Raymond, *Clausewitz: Philosopher of War*, (New Jersey: Prentice-Hall, Inc., Englewood Cliffs, 1985), 81.

main lines along which military events progress, and to which they are restricted, are political lines that continue throughout the war into the subsequent peace."[112]

The reality of reintegration in the midst of war supports Clausewitz's main proposition. Reintegration is an excellent example of the fact that political intercourse with opponents during conflict is not suspended but actually intensified. Reintegration is also evidence for the continuous political intercourse on the war, its objectives, and its conduct within a nation, an alliance or a coalition. These discourses take place with and among the governments, the people, and the military of all countries involved, including the host nation.

It must be stressed that this fundamental insight is not only of theoretical relevance. Reintegration does not only verify the primacy of policies and politics but also that political initiatives set the restrictions for the implementation of violent military means. Reintegration introduced in the midst of a conflict changes the political objectives by placing more emphasis on peace through comprehensive reconciliation. In concert with all means, the military cannot ignore reintegration but must take it into account and, wherever possible, shape its implementation. Since reintegration (like other means employed) is an expression of the overall political purpose, the military has to incorporate its objectives into its strategy, and adjust its own ways and means accordingly–starting at the strategic level and proceeding down to the tactical level. All military ends, ways, and means must be in line with the political logic set by the reintegration effort.

---

[112] Carl von Clausewitz, *On War*, edited and translated by Michael Howard and Peter Paret, (Princeton/New Jersey: Princeton University Press, 1984), 605. Bassford is correct in his statement: "War is an expression of both policy and politics, but 'politics' is the interplay of conflicting forces (inside the state: U.H.), not the execution of one-sided policy initiatives." (Bassword, "Clausewitz and his works", on his webpage
http://www.clausewitz.com/readings/Bassford/Cworks/Works.htm (accessed January 3, 2014). Clausewitz applies this complex understanding of 'Politik' also to the enemy to understand better his intent and his actions: "From the enemy's character, from his institutions, the state of his affairs and his general situation, each side, using the laws of probability, forms an estimate of its opponent's likely course and acts accordingly." (Clausewitz, *On War*, 80). This includes the host nation in case of military interventions. See also Clausewitz, *On War*, 585-586.

4.2 Paradoxical trinity

Realizing that war is based on the interaction among different players, Clausewitz defines war as a "paradoxical trinity". According to his theory, why wars are started, conducted and terminated, and how strategies are developed, decided upon, and implemented, remains predominately the result of three variables that work like magnets, determining the movement of the iron object between them that, in this case, is war. These magnets are (1) the blind natural force of violence, hatred, and enmity; (2) the creative spirit taking advantage of the play of chance and probability, and (3) the rationality that makes war a subordinated instrument of policy.[113]

In Clausewitz's words, "War is more than a true chameleon that slightly adapts its characteristics to the given case. As a total phenomenon its dominant tendencies always make war a paradoxical trinity – composed of primordial violence, hatred, and enmity, which are to be regarded as a blind natural force; of the play of chance and probability within which the creative spirit is free to roam; and of its element of subordination, as an instrument of policy, which makes it subject to reason alone."[114] It is important to acknowledge that Clausewitz regards the comparison with a chameleon that seamlessly adapts to its environment as insufficient, since the totality of interactions may cause radical, unforeseeable changes.

Clausewitz identifies the magnets with social players: (1) the people; (2) the commander and his military forces; and (3) the government. As he argues, "the first of these three aspects (primordial violence, hatred, and enmity) mainly concerns the people; the second (play of chance and probability) the commander and his army; the third (element of subordination) the government. The passions that are to be kindled in war must already be inherent in the people; the scope which the play of courage and talent will enjoy in the realm of probability and chance depends on the particular character of the commander and the army; but the political aims are the business of government alone."[115]

---

[113] Clausewitz, *On War*, 89.

[114] *Ibid.*

[115] *Ibid.*

Characterizing war as a paradoxical trinity (and not just as a chameleon), Clausewitz underlines that the interplay of all social players involved not only relies on their positions but also on their power to enforce them. Their positions and relative advantages may contradict, or reinforce each other. Most importantly, they change constantly.

Reintegration in the midst of a war is also shaped by this trinity.[116] In conceptualizing and implementing reintegration, all strategic leaders have to take the people's emotions into account. During the course of war fighting, emotions are likely to increase when people are directly impacted by violence or indirectly by information, such as reports concerning atrocities transmitted by the news media. The government may be tempted to fuel emotions of the people in order to increase their support of its political objectives; politicians may conclude that the people need enthusiastic victories in order to sustain the war effort. Consequently, emotions may contradict reintegration efforts. On the other side, moral attitudes as well as cultural ties between opponents may be strong enough to convince politicians and people that—in spite of the increasing violence—reintegration is acceptable. The people's war fatigue may also inspire their support for reintegration.

The power of violence, hatred, and enmity can only be overcome by political leaders who have a more peaceful vision and are capable of leading the required change to execute this vision. President Abraham Lincoln may serve as an example of a statesman who expressed his vision of a peaceful U.S. future and the "new birth of freedom" shortly after the battle of Gettysburg in July 1863 that marked the peak of the U.S. Civil War.[117] This speech is also an example of how difficult it is to find understanding, acceptance, and

---

[116] In military interventions, these assessments must be made on three sides: on the side of the host nation, of the intervention states, and those states who are somehow affiliated to insurgents.

[117] It appears to be not unreasonable to compare the APRP with the address of Lincoln on November 19, 1863 with which he tried to reconcile the belligerents in spite of the ongoing U.S. Civil War. He gave a clear vision ("new birth of freedom") and refrained from talking about war crimes, guilt, or from dividing soldiers into two categories (the good and the evil, or the ones with the right cause and others with the wrong cause). Instead, he gave a perspective for a common future.

support amongst the people for a vision of peace in the midst of a conflict.

Military leaders have to advise political leaders on the overall attitudes of the indigenous people, in particular of the insurgents, towards reintegration; in addition, they must ensure that unit leaders maintain discipline of their soldiers who probably have suffered from insurgent activities. Regardless of their own convictions, military leaders need to act creatively in shaping an environment that is supportive to reintegration.[118] Sense of judgment and coup d'oeil (battlefield intuition)[119] are necessary in order to support the implementation of reintegration programs in a complex dynamic political-military environment.

In all these often contradictory interactions within the paradoxical trinity, the government needs to stay committed to making reintegration a political success. In general, reintegration should be initiated as soon as possible, since a continuation of the conflict with increasing violence is likely to lower the acceptability of the reintegration effort. This can be the case for all parties involved: the people, the security personnel, as well as the insurgents. The primacy of policies must be enforced within the military and other government agencies. The military must adapt its strategic end-state as well as its operational approaches to meet better the political objectives of reintegration. The perseverance of strategic leaders is of utmost importance due to the internal tensions within the trinity.

Each nation involved in the conflict has its own trinity and may come up with different conclusions, constraints, and communication strategies on reintegration. Nations may decide not to support reintegration programs or to support such programs financially but instead keep a low profile in their strategic communications with their own populaces and military personnel.

---

[118] The requirements of creative thinking are laid down by Charles D. Allen, "Creative Thinking for Senior Leaders. An essay on creative thinking for military professionals", *US Army War College*, Carlisle, June 2013.
[119] Clausewitz, *On War*, 102.

4.3   Peace

As previously mentioned, due to the primacy of politics and policies, peace, and not military victory, is the ultimate purpose. The envisioned peace must also guide the waging of wars. This proposition is as old as strategic thinking. Strategic military thinkers, ranging from Chinese strategist Sun Tzu and Indian advisor Kautilya to Carl von Clausewitz and Basil Liddell Hart, are in accord, viewing the objective of a better peace in the aftermath of a war as most effective in breaking the cycle of war in foreign affairs.

Sun Tzu pointed out that "there has never been a protracted war from which a country has benefited." He demanded the limiting of the use of force to the greatest extent possible, citing among other elements of this limitation the mandate to treat all captives well. He even requested giving the enemy a chance to escape during sieges. His argument is as follows: "Now you have massed troops and encircled the enemy, who is determined to fight to the death. This is no strategy! You should lift the siege. Let them know that an escape route is open and they will flee and disperse. Then any village constable will be able to capture them!"[120] The expected strategic impact of this tactical approach is that violence will be reduced and, thus, the subsequent peace less burdened by the interaction of the paradoxicial trinity.

Kautilya served as an advisor on statecraft for an Indian king in the 4th century BC. He wanted his king to become a world conqueror, and he believed in the rule of the strongest and in eternal conflict.[121] His *Artha´s-a stra* is a document of realism and considered as an early version of Machiavellianism. German sociologist Max Weber assessed that Machiavelli's book *The Prince* is "harmless" compared to *Artha´s-a stra*.[122] Kautilya assumed that every ruler acts to maximize power and self-interest without any respect for ethical considerations. Consequently, he advised the use of assassinations of

---

[120] Sun Tzu, *The Art of War*. Translated and with an Introduction by Samuel B. Griffith, London/Oxford/New York: Oxford University Press, 1971), 73, 76, 79.

[121] Roger Boesche, "Kautilya's *Arthasastra* on War and Diplomacy in Ancient India," *The Journal of Military History* 67, no. 1 (January 2003): 9-37).

[122] Max Weber, "Politics as a Vocation," in Max Weber, *Selections in Translation*, ed. W. G. Runciman, trans. Eric Matthews (Cambridge: Cambridge University Press, 1978), 220.

neighboring states' leaders and other infamous means to achieve the desired political objectives. On the other hand, with respect to ordinary enemy soldiers and subjects, he thought the best policy was to treat them well and recruit them. Kautilya advised that the kings "not use towards them insults, injuries, contemptuous words or reproaches. And after promising them safety, he should favour them like a father."[123] From his point of view, Realpolitik is best served by sparing the people from violence to the greatest extent possible.

In his treaty on Perpetual Peace, the German philosopher Immanuel Kant (1724-1804) demanded a very deliberate approach to international relations. He related all military actions to the future peace and stressed that none of the warring states should "countenance such modes of hostility as would make mutual confidence impossible in the subsequent state of peace: such are the employment of assassins (percussores), poisoners (venefici), breach of capitulation, and incitement to reason (perduellio) in the opposing state".[124] This principle is very much opposed to Kautilya's advice. Kant made strategic leaders responsible for the consequences of today's action on tomorrow's peace.

Clausewitz, whom some critics accused of focusing only on battles, clearly favors more political or indirect measures. These include "operations that have direct political repercussions that are designed in the first place to disrupt the opposing alliances, or to paralyze it, that gain us new allies, favorably affect the political scene, etc." Therefore, the Prussian general concludes, "if such operations are possible it is obvious that they can greatly improve our prospects and that they can form a much shorter route to the goal than the destruction of the opposing armies."[125] He advises the use of nonviolent means and the limitation of violence to the greatest extent possible, regardless of whether it is directed against the enemy's government, its military, or its people.

This seems to be quite in line with British strategist Basil Liddell Hart's recommendations (although he very much criticized

---

[123] Boesche, "Kautilya's *Arthasastra* on War and Diplomacy in Ancient India," 19.
[124] Immanuel Kant, *To Perpetual Peace: A philosophical Sketch*, London (Georeg Allen&Unwin LTD.) 1917, 114.
[125] Clausewitz, *On War*, 92-93.

Clausewitz as being the 'apostle of annihilation'). Reflecting upon his experience in the Great War, Liddell Hart developed the *indirect approach* as the main principle of achieving strategic success. He emphasized that the theory of war must also be a theory of peace.[126] However, this indirect approach may lead to a cautious approach in utilizing military force and, at the same time, may trigger inhuman attacks on the civil populace, as in the case of Great Britain during World War II.[127] The justification that the war against Germany was a fight for survival calmed Winston Churchill's growing uneasiness with strategic bombing of Britain's opponent that had previously resulted in his question: "Are we beasts? Are we taking this too far?"[128]

In general, obstacles may hinder the political and military leaders from adopting this advice. Primacy or balance of power considerations, ideology, self-esteem of military leaders or simple emotions and, in particular, the fear of losing the war, public support and elections may have an impact on the conduct of warfare in such a way that a better and sustainable peace is not best served. History provides interesting case studies on this issue.

2.500 years ago, the Greek historian Thucydides describes the processes of strategy development in Athens under the conditions of protracted war in a democracy. He explains the Athenian decision to wage war against Sparta as being taken "under the pressure of three of the strongest motives, fear, honor, and interest." This trinity

---

[126] See Liddell Hart, Basil, *Strategy*, (New York: Penguin Books, 1991); see also the critical comments of Lawrence Freedman, *Strategy. A History*, (Oxford: University Press, 2013), 134-139. According to Freedman, "an indirect approach represented a strategic ideal but one only likely to be realized in very special circumstances." See also Anthony James Joes, who lists outstanding strategic theorists emphasizing peace and not military victory as the ultimate aim (Joes, *Resisting Rebellion*, 8-9).

[127] The British indirect approach to strategy in World War II and the conflicts with the U.S. are described in Mark Stoler, *Allies and Adversaries: The Joint Chiefs of Staff, the Grand Alliance, and U.S. Strategy in World War II*, Chapel Hill (UNC Press) 2006, 102-122; see also Stoler, *George C. Marshall*, 89-108.

[128] Tami D. Biddle, "Winston Churchill and Sir Charles Portal: Their Wartime Relationship," *Air Power Leadership: Theory and Practice*, London: The Stationary Office, 2002, 190.

brings understanding as to why those leaders who had preserved peace for many years, finally decided to go to war.[129]

At the end of the Vietnam War, the U.S. intention to conclude the war through peace negotiations went along with an increased military effort that was designed to enable the U.S. to negotiate from a position of strength and, thus, to prevent a decrease in its international prestige.[130]

Also the opposite of reintegration, that is the extinction of the opponent forces or even the entire populace, may become a strategic goal, if ideology comes into play. Any envisioned "peace through extinction" then escalates the violence, as Nazi-Germany during World War II exemplified. The campaign against Russia was a war to gain "Lebensraum" ("living-space") against "Untermenschen" ("sub-humans") and Jews who were declared a threat to the further existence of the German people. Consequently, the war in the East was interwoven with the killing of the European Jews, and Soviet prisoners of war were put in conditions with very limited chances of survival.[131] German strategic theorist Beatrice Heuser points out that "for atrocities to be committed, it was usually sufficient if only one side saw" war as ideologically motivated.[132]

Most importantly, the obsession with winning a war contributes not only to extending its duration but also to disregarding loss of life and destruction, and the chances for future peace.[133] Looking at the history of war, Heuser highlights that "from Napoleon until Castex and Guderian, a paradigm predominated in which battle was seen as central, inevitable and the only way to bring about a decision,

---

[129] *The Landmark Thucydides. A Comprehensive Guide to the Peloponnesian War*, ed. by. Robert B. Strassler, (New York: Free Press 1996). A critical discussion of Thucydides' understanding of the Peloponnesian war is given by Freedman, *Strategy*, 29-35.

[130] See Henry Kissinger, *Diplomacy*, (New York: Simon&Schuster 1994), 674-701. This also played a role in the process of developing the new U.S. strategy for Afghanistan under President Obama. See Woodward, *Obama's Wars, 167*.

[131] Gray, *On Strategy*, 29; Christian Streit, *Keine Kameraden, Die Wehrmacht und die sowjetischen Kriegsgefangenen 1941-1945*, (Bonn: Dietz, 1997).

[132] Heuser, Beatrice, *The Evolution of Strategy. Thinking War from Antiquity to the Present*, (Cambridge; University Press, 2013), 501-502.

[133] Brodie, *War and Politics*, 25-28. World War I serves as an illustrative example.

with all too little thought given to how a subsequent peace should be secured."[134]

This obsession was not suitable for the longstanding paradigm of industrial war, and is even less suitable today for war amongst the people. As Sir Rupert Smith shows, the U.S. doctrine developed by Weinberger and Powel in the 80s and 90s of the last century aimed at winning fast and decisively.[135] Still, military operations are expected to deliver decisive military victories that resolve a political problem. However, this thinking does not meet the requirements of war amongst the people, which has become the new paradigm of warfare. Information, not fire power, is the decisive currency; and all available instruments of power contribute to the campaign. Consequently, victory is not a clear-cut event any more.

If the war is declared as a crusade, if the policies are too idealistic or if victory is seen as an aim in itself by the strategic leaders, and if the military commanders "place the highest priority on what we do rather than on what will achieve our ultimate object,"[136] the introduction of reintegration in the midst of a conflict may appear as contradiction. It would not be easy to explain the need for reintegration within parliament, to the populace, or to the military personnel. If at a later stage the objectives are downsized and reintegration is offered, there may be a negative impact on the international prestige of involved nations and alliances. Usually, superpowers and great powers are perceived as being capable of successfully pursuing their interests with military means, and the people of democracies may need decisive victories for their national pride as much as soldiers need them for their morale. Even minor issues such as naming conventions play into this. Choice of name can show a stark difference in whether one respects opponents as fighters or whether one denounces them as cowards and terrorists. E.g., the Taliban requested that the opposition „respect the name of the mujahedin and stop calling them with inappropriate names."[137]

---

[134] Heuser, *The Evolution of Strategy. Thinking War from Antiquity to the Present*, 502.

[135] Rupert Smith, *The Utility of Force*, (New York: Random House, 2007), 311.

[136] *Ibid.*, 379.

[137] Amato, "Tribes, Pashtunwali and how they impact reconciliation and reintegration efforts in Afghanistan," 31. With respect to reintegration, Joes underlines the

In the case of Afghanistan after 9/11, the U.S. prestige and its strategic culture interwoven with the feelings of revenge and desire for the deterrence of more terrorist attacks led to the policy decision to disregard negotiations with the Taliban leadership and remove it from government.[138] On the Afghan side, reintegration of Taliban fighters was not considered in the initial DDR programs. In addition, the political decision to establish a modern democracy in Afghanistan[139] was hardly compatible with any reintegration or reconciliation efforts with the Taliban, which were widely perceived as "medieval". It would have been almost impossible for any government to justify, and for the people to accept, why these insurgents should be offered the chance to become full members of social communities without being defeated militarily and otherwise punished for their actions. Moreover, the downsizing of the political and military objectives in Afghanistan during the development of a new strategy in 2009[140] made it easier for the IC to accept and support the APRP. In fact, reintegration as introduced in 2010 may better serve an enduring peace in Afghanistan due to its comprehensive approach that links security with good governance and development, as well as aiming at grievance resolution and reconciliation. The IC's support of APRP clearly indicates that its previous strategy in Afghanistan was not working[141] and that military victory should no longer be considered an appropriate objective for the military operations of the U.S. and NATO.

In general, nations that intervene in conflicts should critically analyze whether their strategies promote peace in the host nation, the larger region, and even worldwide, or whether they predominately satisfy their own national interests. Reintegration (integral to reconciliation) as a preferable strategic alternative to military victory must

---

importance of avoiding the word 'surrender'. The reintegration must be an honorable process. See Joes, *Resisting Rebellion*, 167.

[138] See Rumsfeld, *Known and Unknown*, 368.

[139] As announced at the Petersberg Conference in December 2001. The conference is documented on the webpage http://www.unric.org/de/frieden-und-sicherheit/26328 (accessed January 4, 2014).

[140] See chapter 3.5.

[141] See the arguments of Millen, "Time for a Strategic and Intellectual Pause in Afghanistan", 33-45.

be assessed early on to decipher whether it is a more feasible, suitable, and acceptable way to sustainable peace–even if military superiority is a given and victory appears to be likely. From this point of view, reintegration—with its focus on the underlying causes of conflicts and its conflict resolution and reconciliation approaches on all levels of the host nation—can contribute to the critical challenging of one's own strategic assumptions and biases.[142]

4.4   Strategic Culture

Strategic culture is a set of shared traditions, beliefs, assumptions, and habits applied in dealing with security challenges, in particular in using or threatening the use of force.[143] The term comprises more than simply the way a nation fights its wars; rather, it is as comprehensive as the intercourse within the nation's paradoxical trinity.[144] Consequently, strategic culture impacts political and military decisions.

Within a strategic culture, specific images of war may prevail that focus on a specific approach to military operations. The American way of war appears to be value driven "crusades against evil" that focus primarily on absolute victories achieved by annihilation and attrition and are based on its unthreatened industrial underpinnings that provide superior technology and sustained logistics. As General

---

[142] Assumptions and biases do always exist but are not easy to overcome. Several strategic theorists as well as practitioners not only recognize them, but also promote critical thinking to overcome them. See Brodie, *War and Politics*, 1-28; Gates, *Duty*, 589-592. Clausewitz's *On War* can be read as an introduction in critical thinking to understand war and warfare better in its changes and contingencies. See Uwe Hartmann, *Carl von Clausewitz and the Making of Modern Strategy*, Potsdam (Miles-Verlag) 2002, 54-58; Claus von Rosen, Uwe Hartmann, "Clausewitz and the Reception in Germany", Reiner Pommerin (ed.), *Clausewitz goes global. Carl von Clausewitz in the 21ˢᵗ Century*, Berlin (Miles-Verlag) 2014, 138-139.

[143] Russell D. Howards highlights the difficulties in agreeing on a definition of strategic culture. See Howard, Russell D., *Strategic Culture*, Joint Special Operations University (The JSOU Press), December 2013, 1-2.

[144] *Ibid.*, 8. It must be highlighted that non-state actors such as Al Qaeda also have a strategic culture. For an analysis of Al Qaeda's strategic culture see Russell, *Strategic Culture*, 55-63.

Douglas MacArthur famously stated during the Korean war: "There is no substitute for victory."[145]

Scholar Antulio J. Echevarria argues that the U.S. does not have a way of war but a way of battle only.[146] This understanding may have fueled or may be the result of what retired U.S. staff officer and scholar Andrew J. Bacevich calls "military metaphysic": the conviction that the military is the cure-all of international relations and security challenges.[147] Robert Gates stresses the danger of this conviction. Reflecting upon war in his memoirs, the former U.S. Secretary of Defense concludes: "And presidents need to be more willing and skilful in using tools in the national security kit other than hammers. Our foreign and national security policy has become too militarized, the use of force too easy for the president."[148]

Strategic cultures may affect the military mind by focusing on the vision of war that is most "comfortable". Fred Kaplan reconstructs the difficulties General Petraeus and his followers faced when they tried to change the paradigm of warfare within the U.S. Army and to refocus on counterinsurgencies, which had been neglected after the Vietnam War.[149] Russel D. Howard points out that strategic culture can change over time, and that within a given strategic culture, conflicting paradigms may compete.[150] On the other side, strategic cultures may not be flexible enough to recognize and understand the changing character of war. As strategist Hew Strachan underlines, "Although strategic culture uses history to shape its understanding of strategic practice, it is insufficiently attentive to change and contingency, while at the same time being in danger of not fully acknowledging the true source of the continuities which underpin its propositions: that is, geography more than culture."[151]

---

[145] Quoted in Brodie, *War and Politics*, 4.

[146] Echevarria II, Antulio J., *Toward an American Way of War*, Strategic Studies Institute, Carlisle, March 2004.

[147] Andrew J. Bacevich, *The new American Militarism,* Oxford (University Press) 2005, 2.

[148] Gates, *Duty*, 591.

[149] Kaplan, *The Insurgents.*

[150] See Howard, *Strategic Culture*, 9.

[151] Strachan, *The Direction of War*, 7.

In the end, strategic culture is not the silver bullet that prede-termines the desirable strategic effect.[152] Yet, it contributes to a better understanding of the opponent forces, the host nation, allies and partners, and most importantly, of oneself.

Scholars who emphasize the significance of strategic culture often refer to Sun Tzu's prescription to "know the enemy and know yourself; in a hundred battles you will never be in peril".[153] Indeed, the concept of strategic culture may be a proper way to foster critical thinking within the nation's strategic community. In particular, it may help prevent mirror imaging. The U.S. strategic theorist Steven Metz argues that "the long conflict with Iraq demonstrated that the more an opponent is unlike Americans in culture and psychology, the less effective is the U.S. strategy against it. This is true for any nation."[154]

Culture also impacts a nation's and its military's view on rein-tegration. In multinational peace support operations, these cultures may clash–among each other as well as with the culture of the host nation. The Afghan culture of Muslim brotherhood and forgiveness, the American way of war with its preference for annihilation and ultimate defeat of the opponent,[155] and the continental European countries' primacy of civil conflict resolution, each have a unique influence on the respective nations' understanding and support of reintegration. Frictions among different cultures may cause political disputes, uncoordinated military and civil actions with unaligned main efforts, and contradictory strategic communications.[156] Conse-

---

[152] The significance of strategic culture is intensively discussed by Colin S. Gray. See Gray, *Modern Strategy*; Gray, *Perspectives on Strategy*, (Oxford: University Press, 2013), 79-115.

[153] Sun Tzu, *The Art of War*, 84.

[154] Metz, *Iraq & the Evolution of American Strategy*, 193.

[155] The famous proposition of Henry Kissinger "The guerrilla wins if he does not lose. The conventional army loses if it does not win" (Henry Kissinger, „The Viet-nam Negotiations", *Foreign Affairs 47*, 1969, 214) is clearly biased by the U.S. strate-gic culture. In actual fact, based on historical evidence, one may argue that the conventional army must not win but just drain the insurrection. Very early, the strategic theorist Osgood underlined that the U.S. strategic culture is not aligned to waging limited wars. See Robert E. Osgood, *Limited War: The Challenge to American Security*, (Chicago: University of Chicago Press, 1957), 10.

[156] The APRP has been challenged by prejudices from the beginning. Most of them are inspired by cultural biases. Next to wide-spread sceptical assessments on the

quently, it is also important for intervening nations to find out how their own culture is more or less supportive to reintegration.

Strategists underline the role that ethics play in the development and execution of strategies. The German strategic theorist Beatrice Heuser illustrates a "solid tradition stretching from Cicero to the UN that urges princes or other governments not to wage wars that do not fulfill criteria for being 'just'".[157]

The concept of "just war" is a common element of war and morality in many western states.[158] In spite of different interpretations among and within nations, some rules like the *ultima ratio* (i.e., force as the last resort) prescription are taken seriously by strategic leaders, because they are integral to Western values.[159] *Ultima ratio* demands that, if peace is better served by non-violent means, military force is inappropriate and may even be immoral. Strategists are requested to assess carefully whether any ways and means besides the use of military force are available to pursue the political objectives. Thus, if introduced, reintegration with its comprehensive approach must have primacy over military operations. Consequently, ethical principles also request that strategic leaders adjust military ends, ways, and means to meet better the political objectives of reintegration programs.

---

success changes and the exaggerated forecasts on recidivism numbers, many voices have pointed out that the former combatants were only trying to receive government payment. As an example, see Rod Nordland and Alissa J. Rubin, "Taliban impostors vex reintegration plan. Many are believed to be opportunists looking for handouts", *The International Herald Tribune*, February 20, 2012.

[157] Heuser, *The Evolution of Strategy*, 500.

[158] Gray, *Perspectives on Strategy*, 72. See also page 65, where the author argues that "all people seemingly are biologically and psychologically programmed to think morally". See also Gray, *On Strategy*, 12, 26, 73. The role of ethics in the development of modern strategy is also emphasized by Osgood, *Limited War*, 9.

[159] In Germany, ethical scholars and theologians have proposed to replace the 'Just War' theory by the 'Just Peace' concept. In the German armed forces, the leadership philosophy (Innere Führung) has been trying to anchor the soldier's self-understanding in peace, not victory. See Claus von Rosen, "Wissenschaft und Militärische Führung in Baudissins Konzeption Innere Führung", *Jahrbuch Innere Führung 2013. Wissenschaften und ihre Relevanz für die Bundeswehr als Armee im Einsatz*, ed. by Uwe Hartmann and Claus von Rosen, (Berlin: Miles-Verlag 2013), 87.

Due to the interlinked security, diplomatic, intelligence, development, and justice dimensions of reintegration, any activities to support reintegration efforts should be based on the whole-of-government approach. This approach characterizes the security policy in many western states as well as in NATO. The need for this approach can be related to strategic thought. Clausewitz's insight into war as a continuation of policies and politics with other means makes clear that war is based on the intercourse of all agencies of the government.

However, the strategic culture within nations is not always entirely supportive of the implementation of this policy.[160] In addition, the host nation may also struggle with the execution of reintegration programs due to its own nascent capacities and capabilities. Reintegration suffers as a result, but, on the other hand, may still serve as an effective catalyst for improving the interagency and intragovernmental as well as the intergovernmental cooperation.

The military culture within armed forces must also be taken into account. The longer the individual is part of a specific culture, the more the assumptions and values of this culture are hardwired, therefore causing resistance to change.[161] If a soldier's DNA is programmed for war fighting, it is unlikely that the soldier will understand the ends and ways of reintegration and creatively conduct military action in its support. This programming may be a reason, particularly among military personnel, for the widespread scepticism and the prejudices against the APRP.[162]

It is becoming increasingly apparent that it is of vital importance to have forces at hand that are culturally specified to cooperate

---

[160] Raymond A. Millen and Carolyn Pruitt describe the deficiencies in the implementation of the comprehensive approach in stability operations and develop a proposal to overcome major organizational challenges. See Raymond A. Millen, Carolyn Pruitt, "The Government Assistance Center: A Vehicle for Transitioning to the Host Government", *PKSOI Papers*, Carlisle, May 2011. See also Metz, Steven, *Iraq & the Evolution of American Strategy*, 179.

[161] See Stephen J. Gerras, Leonard Wong, Charles D. Allen, "Organizational Culture: Applying A Hybrid Model to the U.S. Army," *US Army War College*, Strategic Leadership, Volume III (2013).

[162] Some authors voiced their concerns that recidivism will occur in large numbers, such as Jones, "Reintegrating Afghan Insurgents," 13; Johnson, "Reintegration and Reconciliation in Afghanistan," 100.

closely with indigenous military and civilian personnel in conflict areas. For instance, the U.S. armed forces developed the "Afghan Hands" program to make available specifically trained personnel in support of the APRP;[163] and the U.S. Special Forces were instrumental in building up the Afghan Local Police (ALP).[164]

Changing the mindset of military personnel of the conventional forces, in particular, with regard to this issue is difficult. As analyst Linda Robinson points out, conventional forces did not realize that the main effort of the new U.S. strategy was placed on the successful build-up of the ALP.[165]

The emphasis on the human dimension of war that characterizes the current transformation of the U.S. armed forces is now being understood as a necessary response to the significance of culture in war and warfare. Such an emphasis also helps to utilize non-violent means better in modern conflicts that, as British General Sir Rupert Smith argues, will often be "war amongst the people."[166]

The re-discovered human dimension of war is based on the insight that the paradoxical trinity of war predominately takes place on the land. The land is where the people, the government, and the military primarily interact. This interaction must be influenced in accordance with national interests. All domains contribute to affecting the enemy's will; however, the land domain's impact remains the most decisive.[167]

Nevertheless, if the military frame of reference is not directed towards peace (but only linked to national interests and strategic cultures), greater emphasis placed on the human dimension of war will not be sufficient to gain a better understanding of the opportunities possible with reintegration nor to incorporate reintegration into one's own intellectual understanding of warfare. Otherwise, the human

---

[163] More information on the Afghan hands is available at http://www.jcs.mil/page.aspx?id=52 (accessed January 4, 2014).

[164] See Robinson, *One Hundred Victories*.

[165] *Ibid.*, 86, 102. Fred Kaplan describes the difficulties of General McChrystal as commander of ISAF to implement COIN. See Kaplan, *The Insurgents*, 325-327.

[166] Smith, *The Utility of Force*.

[167] The discussions within the U.S. armed forces on the human domain as the 7th warfighting function are reflected in Cleveland, Charles T., Farris, Stuart L., "Landpower," *Army*, July 2013, 20-23.

domain would be merely a new technique, and not a way to comprehend better the utility of force.

It is not easy for military personnel, be they members of the host nation's armed forces, or of the intervention forces, to understand reintegration, particularly in its complex and complicated connection with development and governance. Furthermore, advising the security forces of the host nation on how to conduct and support reintegration and how to deal with local police forces is frequently a delicate matter.

4.5 Limited War

Clausewitz explains why, in theory, war has the tendency to escalate.[168] Intensively analyzing history, he realized that wars often occurred in rather limited forms. In limited wars, belligerents may attempt to achieve decisive or ultimate results; however, they constrain the ways and means involved in achieving ends for various reasons.[169] During the course of the war, governments may reconsider this and further escalate or de-escalate war efforts. Consequently, the conduct of war shapes policy, and political objectives are likely to be redefined.

It is worthwhile to highlight this insight. From today's perspective, World War I and World War II, two conflicts that were unlimited to the greatest extent possible, are the historical exception rather than the rule. However, they still dominate the perception of war as observed by all social actors within the paradoxical trinity throughout many countries.[170]

In the early phases of the Cold War, limited wars appeared to be feasible and winnable wars. Strategist Robert Osgood defined limited war as "one in which the belligerents restrict the purposes for which they fight to concrete, well-defined objectives that do not demand the utmost military effort of which the belligerents are capable and that can be accommodated in a negotiated settlement."[171] They

---

[168] Clausewitz, *On War*, 77.

[169] *Ibid.*, 222. See also Strachan, *The Direction of War*, 13.

[170] See Max Boot, *Invisible Armies. An Epic History of Guerrilla Warfare from Ancient Times to the Present,* (New York/London: Liveright Publishing Corporation, 2013).

[171] Osgood, *Limited War*, 4.

permit the economic, social, and political life of a country to continue without serious disruption. Osgood highlighted the need of combining military power with diplomacy and with the economic and psychological instruments of power, and proposed the interagency or whole-of-government approach. However, Osgood underestimated the role of the military in the development of strategies. He also did not foresee how states in future would struggle to define and redefine the objectives they pursue during limited wars.

Limited war can be characterized as limited only in hindsight. One never knows in advance how war will develop, because its ends may change. An historical example is the Korean War, in which the United States and its coalition partners abandoned its objective of defeating North Korea when China intervened. Other conflicts, such as the Vietnam War, were limited on one side but not on the other: While the Vietcong waged an unlimited war, the United States was not willing to continue escalating the war beyond a specific point.[172] Such examples lead to the conclusion that it is not easy to define one's own goals, if the goal of the other side is not clear or subject to change; and it is not easy to limit one's goals if the irregular forces, as a necessity, must wage guerrilla warfare. Colin S. Gray highlights that „guerrilla warfare is the character of warfare waged of necessity by irregular belligerents".[173] If that is the case, any assessment on the level of war is rather difficult.

While wars can have different political ends that range from extremely limited and unlimited to the greatest extent possible, there is only one means: that is combat. As Clausewitz argues, "Whenever armed forces, that is armed individuals, are used, the idea of combat must be present."[174] That does not mean, however, that combat must always take place, and that belligerents must strive for the most destructive means available when conducting combat. Nonetheless, as Clausewitz illustrates, "if one of the two commanders is resolved to seek a decision through major battles, he will have an excellent chance of success if he is certain that his opponent is pursuing a dif-

---

[172] At that time, the primary opponent was the Soviet Union.
[173] Colin S. Gray, „Irregular warfare: Guerrillas, insurgents and terrorists", in *War, Peace and International relations*, (London: Routledge, 2007), 251
[174] Clausewitz, *On War*, 95.

ferent policy. Conversely, the commander who wishes to adopt different means can reasonably do so only if he assumes his opponent to be equally unwilling to resort to major battles."[175] Consequently, a strategic leader needs to „... keep an eye on his opponent so that he does not, if the latter has taken up a sharp sword, approach him armed only with an ornamental rapier."[176]

This strategic insight is of utmost importance for those conducting reintegration during wars. In general, reintegration has a better chance of being implemented successfully in limited rather than in higher intensity conflicts. Since reintegration progress is dependent on the perception of the security situation by the people–and war may escalate, if this is the opponents' intent –it needs to be accompanied by effective military force.[177] Strategists should be aware that reintegration cannot replace the use or threat of violence; it is not a stand-alone instrument to achieve political ends in a war zone. Even in very limited wars, reintegration is not a recipe for subduing the enemy *without fighting*, as Sun Tzu defined the acme of skill.[178] The capability of the host country and the intervention forces to fight successfully and the perception of this capability by the people are essential in order to gain the insurgents' willingness to reintegrate.[179] Reintegration will only achieve its objectives, if the utility of force is given and clearly expressed. If these preconditions are met, reintegration may be in line with Basil Liddell Hart's main proposition that the true aim of the strategist "… is not so much to seek battle as to seek a strategic situation so advantageous that if it does not of itself produce the decision, its continuation by a battle is sure to achieve

---

[175] *Ibid.*, 98.

[176] *Ibid.*, 99; see also 76.

[177] The use of coercive power in diplomacy was developed by the economist Thomas S. Schelling. See Thomas C. Schelling, "The Diplomacy of Violence," in *Arms and Influence* (New Haven, CT: Yale University Press, 1966), 1-6, 12-34.

[178] Sun Tzu, *The Art of War*, 77. Also, Basil Liddell Hart advocates bloodless victories as the ultimate goal of strategy.

[179] The reliance on military power comes along with the interest of superpowers, great powers or alliances not to lose wars, even if wars are limited and not related to vital interests. It is the perception of weakness with its implications for the international system that determines the interest of nations not winning wars.

this."[180] Looking at Clausewitz's own propositions, it is reasonable to suggest that he and Liddell Hart would have agreed upon this.

4.6   Counterinsurgency (COIN)

COIN is the understanding of the theory and practice of irregular warfare and insurgencies by the militarily superior power that fights them.[181] It is a highly complex operational approach that synchronizes political, economic, and military ends, ways and means. Political ends, ways, and means must be the 'superior intelligence' since "guerrilla insurgency is quintessentially a political phenomenon, and that therefore any effective response to it must be primarily political as well."[182] However, author Fred Kaplan, referring to past conflicts, drew this conclusion, "If one of the elements was zero, the product of all three would be zero; that is, if one prong of the operation failed, the entire campaign could fail, and thus the insurgents would win."[183]

In the overall calculation, the ratio between the non-military and military ways and means is 80:20%. This has been articulated from Mao Zedong to modern COIN theorists and practitioners. The complicated arrangement of the various ends, ways and means is one of the reasons why British Colonel T. E. Lawrence who became famous as "Lawrence of Arabia", compared COIN to "eating soup with a knife".

In COIN operations, people are the main focus. Their primacy is highlighted in the definition of irregular warfare given by the U.S. Armed Forces. COIN is understood as a "violent struggle

---

[180] Liddell Hart, *Strategy*, 339.

[181] Anthony James Joes highlights some deficiencies in understanding insurgencies. If understood as "a scaled-down version of conventional war, if its political and strategic impacts are not respected and knowledge of counterinsurgencies is ignored, governments and armed forces may face severe consequences." (Joes, *Resisting Rebellion*, 1-9).

[182] Joes, *Resisting Rebellion*, 7.

[183] Kaplan, *The Insurgents*, 19. See also John A. Nagl, *Learning to eat Soup with a Knife: Counterinsurgency Lessons from Malaya and Vietnam*, London and Chicago (University of Chicago Press) 2005.

among state and non-state actors for legitimacy and influence over the relevant populations."[184]

Within the academic and military discourses, two ways are discussed by which to win the support of the people: the "hearts and minds" approach vs. the "incentive/disincentive" approach. As analyst Austin Long proposes, a combination of both may best serve political objectives. "It would appear that acknowledging that humans actually follow both logics simultaneously would be a good first step. Incentives clearly do matter to humans, driving many decisions in daily life. Yet preferences, particularly those that involve the legitimacy or illegitimacy of an action, quite obviously affect decision-making as well. The interaction of microlevel incentives with personal conceptions of identity and legitimacy probably provide the best guide to action".[185]

While most of the insurgencies were not successful, the overall historical record of COIN is also less than promising. Fighting the "myth of the invincible guerrilla" affecting U.S. policy,[186] some theorists and practitioners highlight opportunities for successful COIN operations.[187] This attempt has been countered recently as well. Fundamental opposition against COIN has been emerging as a reaction to the proclaimed successes in Iraq that have been mainly contributed to COIN as executed by General Petraeus. Referring to the experience of COIN in Afghanistan, Fred Kaplan supports the conclusion of COIN-expert David Kilcullen that "unless there is a reasonable likelihood that the affected government will introduce necessary reforms", COIN would be "folly".[188] He not only makes a strong argument that COIN is not suitable for Afghanistan but also

---

[184] See the U.S. Joint Chiefs of Staff, JP-1, *Doctrine for the Armed Forces of the United States*, (Washington D.C.: Joint Chiefs of Staff), March 25, 2013, I-6.

[185] See Austin Long, "On 'Other War'. Lessons from Five Decades of RAND Counterinsurgency", *RAND Corporation 2006*, 21-33. Another disagreement exists on the calculation of COIN forces: should their size be based on counterinsurgent-to-insurgent or counterinsurgent-to-population ratios. See Millen, "Time for a Strategic and Intellectual Pause in Afghanistan," 37.

[186] *Ibid.*, 247.

[187] Kaplan, *The Insurgents,* 19.

[188] *Ibid.*, 341. See also Jian Gentile, "COIN is Dead: U.S. Army Must Put Strategy Over Tactics," *Small Wars Journal*, November 22, 2011. In fact, insurgencies are often caused by bad governance.

makes this conclusion from other historical examples: "In counterinsurgency wars, it's not just the enemy that has a vote; the ally does, too. If you send troops overseas to bolster a regime whose leaders lack legitimacy or the will to reform, the most brilliant strategy–and strategist–will have little chance of prevailing. Counterinsurgency is a technique, not a grand strategy."[189] This, again, highlights Clausewitz's main proposition that war is a continuation of policies and politics. COIN is not only subordinated to the superior intelligence of policies and politics but also relies on the successful pursuit of political ends, ways, and means.

Challenging the ways to win the support of the people, scholar Raymond Millen argues that "it is difficult to discern how the Hearts-and-Minds enhances government legitimacy."[190] The COIN critique of historian Douglas Porch is even more fundamental. Analyzing several historical COIN cases, he points out that success was not achieved by "hearts and minds" or "incentive/disincentive" approaches. Instead he argues that, in fact, COIN forces used extreme violence against the people in order to separate them from the insurgents.[191] Porch concludes that "each insurgency is a contingent event in which doctrine, operations, and tactics must support a viable policy and strategy, not the other way around."[192] The usage of COIN tactics alone is not likely to generate the desired strategic outcome.[193]

Reintegration can be seen as essential to COIN. As Major General Hook, the 2nd FRIC in ISAF Headquarters argues: "Any counterinsurgency strategy includes a nonmilitary solution that reaches out to insurgents with the goal of peaceful reintegration where everyone benefits."[194] The utility of reintegration is also supported by the COIN mathematics, as promoted by General

---

[189] Kaplan, *The Insurgents,* 39, 362.

[190] Millen, "Time for a Strategic and Intellectual Pause in Afghanistan," 36.

[191] Kaplan, *The Insurgents,* 39, 364; Porch, *Counterinsurgency,* 153-200.

[192] Douglas Porch, *Counterinsurgency. Exposing the Myths of the New Way of War,* (Cambridge: University Press, 2013), xii.

[193] *Ibid.,* 320.

[194] Cited in Cheryl Pellerin, "Afghan Insurgent Reintegration Effort Works, Official Says, *U.S. Department of Defense Information,* 22 Feb 2012). See also Jones, "Reintegrating Afghan Insurgents", 19; see also the deficiencies in ISAF, as identified by General Petraeus and General McChrystal (Woodward, *Obama's* Wars, 17, 165).

McChrystal. "Killing an insurgent may make enemies of his father, sons, brothers and friends, whereas removing the cause for conflict does not."[195] Intending to implement COIN in Afghanistan, General MyChrystal and General Petraeus identified significant deficiencies in the field of reintegration. The relevance of reintegration for COIN does not suggest that it can only be implemented within this specific operational approach. In fact, reintegration can be applied to other approaches including high intensity operations as well.

The subordination of reintegration to COIN means ignoring its political objectives, often with destabilizing results. Reintegration should not be a means to COIN but instead COIN should be a means to support reintegration. Reintegration, in order to be successful, must be seen as the overall political concept that directs COIN, which, consequently, must be seen as the supporting activity.

Serving the purposes of reintegration, COIN can elevate itself from a technique with often limited strategic effect to an essential element of a strategy that promotes peace, deescalates violence and improves governance and development.[196] Its effects can be increased still more by reconciliation efforts at the highest political level. Linking and subordinating COIN to reintegration and reconciliation clearly communicates the message that the host nation and its international partners do not intend to wage a general war that pursues decisive military defeat of opponent forces or brutal oppression of the indigenous population, but which strives instead for sustainable peace that involves all. Consequently, the use of force in COIN must be aligned with the overall aim of peace, and thus with the grievance resolution and reconciliation efforts.

This conclusion is supported by Anthony James Joes who argues: "The aim of true counterinsurgency is to reestablish peace. Real peace means reintegrating into society its disaffected elements. The

---

[195] Cited in Alexander, ",Decomposing an Insurgency. Reintegration in Afghanistan'", 50. The reasoning behind the COIN mathematics in Afghanistan is described in Kaplan, The Insurgents, 324.

[196] In Afghanistan, it turned out that the lack of governance was one of the decisive factors in why COIN could not be implemented. See the arguments of former general and then U.S. Ambassador Eikenberry in the decision-making process, as described by Woodward, Obama's Wars, 261-262. See also Kaplan, The Insurgents, 313-315.

rate, even the possibility, of such reintegration depends in great part on how the counterinsurgency was conducted. Reintegration becomes incomparably more likely if the counterinsurgents deliberately choose conservative military tactics, undergirded by serious efforts to limit abuses against the civil population, redress salient grievances, make amnesty attractive, and erect a legitimate government."[197]

---

[197] Joes, *Resisting Rebellion*, 246.

5 Wag the Dog: Military Operations in Support of Reintegration

Reintegration is a political program that interrelates with the military, since it takes fighters from the battlefield, thus improving the overall force ratio, and it engages the population, thus contributing to COIN. Consequently, it is in the military's interest that reintegration programs are conducted successfully.

What can the military do to support the implementation of reintegration programs? First of all, and most importantly, the military must adjust its strategies to meet better the political purposes of reintegration (and reconciliation) programs introduced during conflicts. In order to become relevant and practical, the revised military strategies must be translated into operational plans and tactical actions. Consequently, the military has to incorporate reintegration in its operational plans and tactical orders.

Military means can be supportive to the host nation's and the IC's reintegration efforts, if applied in a specific way.

1) If military operations are perceived as successful, insurgents (and/or those who ordered them to become insurgents due to hedging behavior or contribution to the family income) may realize that they will benefit more from changing sides than continuing to fight; or that hedging is not necessary any longer and/or other job opportunities offer better income. Quite often, both the deployment of holding forces[198] and the installation of checkpoints in specific areas are necessary to enforce the perception of a military operation being successful. Military short- and long-term planning should incorporate the fielding of holding forces as a major component of the reintegration progress.

2) The creation of national holding forces to secure the area, thus replacing national security and/or international forces, is extremely important also for operational success. As Max Boot argues, „The only way to gain control is to garrison troops 24 hours a day, seven days a week, among the civil-

---

[198] Holding forces can be ALP or elements of the ANSF and/or ISAF.

ians; periodic 'sweep' or 'cordon and search' operations fail, even when conducted by counterinsurgents as cruel as the Nazis, because civilians know that the rebels will return the moment the soldiers leave."[199] One may argue that military clearing operations will only be successful if holding forces are deployed. On reintegration, the deployment of holding forces has a threefold impact: They clearly indicate the commitment to providing long-term security, they prevent the insurgents' return after the termination of the military operations, and they attract former combatants by offering opportunities to apply for jobs after successful reintegration.

3)   In addition to providing security with holding forces, it is important that the government at the district and, if possible, also at the province and even state level becomes visibly involved in improving the livelihood of the people. The national security forces and the administration at the different levels must conduct activities in line with the comprehensive approach, supported by the IC and IOs/NGOs. Consequently, security forces of the host nation need a CIMIC capability that should not only be regarded as a contributing factor to Force Protection but also as a capacity to improve governance and development.[200] The comprehensive approach with the allocation of significant resources is particularly needed in those districts, in which the insurgency has taking control.

4)   Thorough investigations of the reasons for grievances in villages are necessary to understand the people better as well as the insurgents and their motivation to fight.[201] National peace committees in close cooperation with intelligence services support the conflict parties to settle internal grievances. IOs and NGOs may also become involved. It is of utmost impor-

---

[199] Max Boot, "The Evolution of Irregular War: Insurgents and Guerrillas From Akkadia to Afghanistan," *Foreign Affairs*, 92.2 (Mar/Apr 2013), 100-114.

[200] However, this raises the question on how far military security forces should get involved in civil affairs.

[201] For Afghanistan, see the article "Understanding & Communicating. Neutralizing the ARGHANDAB River Valley insurgency" in: *COIN*, Volume 3, Issue 1, April 2012, 5-6.

tance that the officials at the different levels publicly commit to resolving grievances. They may be required to provide land or other means of compensation to help resolve these grievances. International forces should not be involved in this process; however, military intelligence may contribute to analyzing grievances. Timings and locations of reintegration efforts (outreach, demobilization, reintegration) as well as grievance resolution activities should be taken into account by the military planners; this requires their close cooperation with the host nation as well as with civil partners.

5) Special Forces operations support reintegration by taking out the insurgents' leaders or ideologically motivated fighters. If leaders are taken out, their followers may become more inclined to consider reintegration. Specially designed information operations should be used when trying to influence their decision-making process. However, it appears to be beneficial also to address specific leaders and convince them to reintegrate, particularly since the opportunity is provided for them to reintegrate together with their followers. In the end, violent action against low- or mid-level commanders must not be conducted too extensively or unlinked with reintegration efforts, since killed or captured commanders may be replaced by younger leaders who are even more ideologically inclined. Those who are assessed as willing to reintegrate, should be removed from target lists.[202]

6) Overall, the use of military violence should be restricted to the greatest extent possible. The more violence has occurred, the less successful reintegration may be. From the perspective of the individual insurgent, it is more difficult to decide to accept the reintegration offer the longer he has been fighting. This may be one of the more important reasons for the reintegration successes in RC North, where, compared with other regions, most former combatants had been fighting less than one year at the time of their reintegration application.[203]

---

[202] Johnson, "Reintegration and Reconciliation in Afghanistan," 98.
[203] Humphreys, Macartan, Weinstein, Jeremy M., "Demobilization and reintegration", *The Journal of Conflict Resolution*, Vol. 51, No. 4 (Aug., 2007), 531-567.

7)   Information operations and special operations should be coordinated with the host nation's intelligence services as well as with the local reintegration (and reconciliation) officials, if possible.

8)   Information operations[204] are vital in influencing the perception of the people/insurgents. Target audiences should be defined depending on the culture. In Afghanistan, the Imams and Mullahs as well as the wifes of insurgents are essential audiences that may be more susceptible to Western views.[205] The youth are yet another audience that may play an important role in this process.[206] However, the success of information operations relies on real progress in the livelihood of the people (including the former combatants). It is important that community projects are quickly initiated once the military operations are concluded.

9)   Military commanders should engage political and religious leaders and encourage them to support the reintegration efforts to the greatest extent possible.

The military also needs to take the reactions of the insurgents' leadership into account. If reintegration succeeds, the insurgents will try to discredit reintegration through propaganda and through coercion: they will likely kill reintegrated former insurgents and punish communities that receive them. In addition, they will improve their own grievance resolution capabilities, and may even attempt to channel still active insurgents into the reintegration process (and also into the local security forces, if established).[207]

Since the host nation leads the execution of the reintegration program, the national security forces at the same time must lead the

---

[204] On the significance of information operations in modern warfare see T. X. Hammes, "Fourth Generation Warfare Evolves, Fifth Emerges," *Military Review*, 87.3 (May/Jun 2007), 14-23.

[205] The importance of religion in stability operations is discussed in Matyók, Thomas, Flaherty, Maureen, Tuso, Hamdesa, Senehi, Jessica, Byrne, Sean (eds.), *Peace on Earth. The Role of Religion in Peace and Conflict Studies*, Lanham (Lexington Books) 2013.

[206] Musa/Morgan/Keegan, "Policing and COIN Operations. Lessons Learned, Strategies and Future Directions," 99.

[207] Jones, "Reintegrating Afghan Insurgents," 15.

planning and execution of military operations conducted in support of reintegration. However, their military leaders may be even more hesitant to support reintegration than the personnel of the armed forces of intervention states, due to their often greater sufferings from violence or political and ideological inclinations. The longer the war lasts, the more difficult reintegration becomes: because soldiers and the people are more emotional, because grievances have increased, and because enmities between political parties, religious communities, or ethnicities have been fueled. Even if the culture of a country is supportive of reintegration, the military's specific culture may be different. This can potentially become even more complicated if grievances are created by the security forces of the host nation, by the intervention forces, or by political authorities. In such circumstances, it would be a very delicate task for mentors or advisors from intervention forces to change those elements of the host nation's military culture that are not aligned with the objective of reintegration and reconciliation.

How should the military staffs be organized to incorporate reintegration into their planning activities? First, the issue of reintegration must be a focal point of military education and training. For this purpose, the doctrines have to be adapted to comprise reintegration in the midst of a conflict.[208] Second, staffs must have elements that are powerful enough to bring this issue into the staff work. The intelligence divisions should focus on low- and mid-level commanders, their men, their supporters, and potential ways to encourage or coerce them to reintegrate. Since reintegration is a field of civil-military cooperation, the military element should be closely attached to the staff elements of civilian partners, in particular the Senior Civil Representatives and development officials of the troop contributing nations. Extremely important is the cooperation between the Special Forces and Conventional Forces, and their respective staff elements. Thus, in general, the headquarters' division responsible for reintegration should be well-known to the staff and well-versed in the staff work, rather than an unfamiliar outsider.

---

[208] ADRP 3-07 *Stability*, Headquarters, Department of the Army, August 2012. See Annex 4 of this book.

6 Square the Circle: Civil-military Relations, Interagency Cooperation and Reintegration

A clear-cut divide between the civil and the military domains in war and warfare is not possible. Collaboration between these domains does cause tension but, more importantly, it requires that both domains cooperate closely. Prerequisite to such a collaboration is the honest attempt of all stakeholders to try to understand their partners' and their own interests, cultures, assumptions, and biases.

Clausewitz underlines the overall political character of war. His fundamental insight on war as a continuation of polices and politics is the result not only of his theoretical deliberations but also of his personal contribution to state and war making in Prussia after the decisive defeat of the Prussian army in the battles of Jena and Auerstedt against Napoleon in 1806.[209] He concludes that the delivery of military advice, without touching on the realm of policies and politics, is not possible. He provides this caution: „that a major military development, or the plan for one, should be a matter for *purely military* opinion is unacceptable and can be damaging. Nor indeed is it sensible to summon soldiers ... and ask them for *purely military advice.*"[210]

Due to the fact that all military advice and all military actions are related to policies and politics, the Prussian philosopher of war leaves no doubt where the final responsibility for the development and execution of strategies lies – with the government. Consequently, strategist Bernard Brodie concludes, "we must avoid putting the blame primarily on the military commanders. The responsibility for

---

[209] Clausewitz contributed to the reform of the Prussian state as the assistant to Gerhard von Scharnhorst, the head of the Military Reform Commission. For detailed information, see Gordon A. Craig, *The Politics of the Prussian Army 1640-1945*, London/New York (1955/64): 37-53; Peter Paret, *Clausewitz and the State*, 137-146.

[210] See Clausewitz, *On War*, 607. This was already stated by Sun Tzu, although he requested that politicians stay out of the war-making being conducted by the general. As a consequence, he argues, it is the general himself who has to think in terms of grand strategy, in particular with respect to the impact of warfare on the economy.

their selection and their retention or dismissal is and was ultimately the politician's".[211] This implies also that military leaders have to respect the political objectives in the development of operational designs as well as during the conduct of operations.

Due to enemies having "a vote", to chance and friction,[212] to simple mistakes and miscalculations as well as to changes in the domestic and international environments, strategies have to be adapted constantly. Consequently, permanent interaction between the government and the military leaders based on trustful relations is required in all phases of a war. This interaction should be facilitated by the personalities of all strategic leaders and their advisers as well as through the organization of the security system within a state or alliance.

Nevertheless, as Clausewitz emphasizes, this collaboration and synchronization is never easy to conduct. The various instruments of national power share the same logic given by the establishment of policies and politics as the "superior intelligence", but each of them has its own grammar.[213] Therefore, policy and politics have to respect the peculiarities of their various instruments. Strategy cannot focus on the political objectives alone but must take the grammar of the use of military force into account. This implies, as Clausewitz stresses, that policy and politics are not independent. The political aim "must adapt itself to its chosen means, a process which can radically change it. Policy, then, will permeate all military operations, and, in so far as their violent nature will permit, it will have a continuous influence on them."[214]

Consequently, the guiding intelligence of policy must incorporate a thorough understanding of the nature of war. Political ob-

---

[211] Brodie, *War and Politics*, 27.

[212] Clausewitz, *On War*, 85: „No other human activity is so continuously or universally bound up with chance. And through the element of chance, guesswork and luck come to play a great part in war." See also Clausewitz's considerations of danger, physical exhaustion, lack of information, and friction on pp. 113-121. The significant emphasis of friction is unique to Clausewitz. Sun Tzu did not consider friction. Friction will not occur, as long as his strategic advice is respected by the general.

[213] Brodie, *War and Politics*, 1-2.

[214] Clausewitz, *On War*, 87.

jectives must take the peculiarities of warfare, or, as Clausewitz puts it, its grammar, into account. Politicians also need to understand that warfare will *constantly* shape their policies and politics. These are more than likely to change before the termination of the war. Therefore, strategy must serve as a bridge between the two worlds of the politicians and the military leaders; it must be the glue, as Hew Strachan describes, which binds the political objectives to the military capabilities.[215] In addition, the communicative skills of all involved, in particular the political leaders, are essential to the transformation of the "unequal dialogue"[216] into a discourse that prevents manipulation and dominance but enhances trust, self-awareness, partnership, curiosity, and mutual critical thinking.[217]

The development of strategies as the alignment of political objectives with military ends, ways, and means is prone to conflict. Analyzing recent wars and conflicts, several scholars highlight this insight. The most prominent of these scholars, Hew Strachan, argues: "By confusing strategy with policy and by calling what were in reality political effects strategic effects, governments denied themselves the intellectual tool to manage war for political purposes, and so allowed themselves to project their daily political concerns back into strategy."[218] Thus, the British strategist emphasizes deficits on the side of the politicians.

Often, political leaders do not fully understand that the nature of war is characterized not only by violence, but also by unpredictability and poor controllability. Unrealistically, they tend to expect that definitive military victories will resolve political problems.[219] Military leaders, particularly commanders in the field, sense this lack

---

[215] Strachan, *The Direction of War*, 12; see also Smith, *The Utility of Force*, 375.

[216] Eliot A. Cohen, *Supreme Command. Soldiers, Statesmen, and Leadership in Wartime*, New York (Anchor Books) 2003, 208-224.

[217] The communication skills required in discourses are described in John P. Kotter, *Leading Change*, Boston (Harvard Business Review Press) 2012, 87-104. The requirements of critical thinking for strategic leaders are laid down in Stephen J. Gerras, "Thinking Critically about Critical Thinking: a Fundamental Guide for Strategic Leaders," *US Army War College*, Carlisle, August 2008. See also Tami Davis Biddle, "Grand Strategy: Art of the Possible, or Impossible Art?" *US Army War College,* 16-22.

[218] Strachan, *The Direction of War*, 21.

[219] Smith, *The Utility of Force*, 375.

of understanding and deficit of strategic guidance, and are tempted or compelled to develop their own desired strategic effects. If these issues are not discussed in an open, trustful way, and if institutions responsible for the development of strategies are not capable of serving as a bridge between policy and operations, then conflicts and tensions will be unavoidable. In the end, the political and military divide will become deeper.

Nonetheless, there are also some positive developments with respect to strategy making. Since the end of the Cold War, political and military leaders have learned from harsh experience that they cannot achieve their political objectives solely with military means. In fact, the need for blending political, economic, development, informational and military instruments had previously been a lesson learned from colonial warfare. However, in the military systems of western states, this has not become paradigmatic. By contrast, doctrine was predominately focused on major battles of annihilation. With the end of the Cold War and the beginning of numerous peace-keeping or stability operations in failing or failed states, the military has become the driving force in pushing for more intra-governmental collaboration.

In the first decade of the 21st century, all major western countries introduced or re-emphasized the whole-of-government or comprehensive approach.[220] This reflects the challenges imposed by the increasing complexity of conflicts. The shared assumption is that complexity can be best met by improved cooperation among the state's agencies, between different states, and with International Organizations (IO) and Non-governmental Organizations (NGO). Simultaneously, the significance of Grand or National Strategies has been highlighted. The term goes back to Basil Liddell Hart and is defined as the employment of all instruments of national power to achieve political objectives.[221]

Seen through the eyes of Carl von Clausewitz, the whole-of-government approach, as argued above, is challenged by friction. Representatives of the military cannot give purely military advice.

---

[220] Going beyond intra-governmental collaboration, the comprehensive approach includes IOs and NGOs. It is also the overarching policy in NATO.
[221] Liddell Hart, *Strategy*.

When interacting with politicians or leaders of civil organizations, military personnel will always touch the realms and responsibilities of their partners. In addition, all stakeholders involved are biased towards giving assessments from the point of view of their respective organizations. In other words, "where you stand is where you sit." To overcome different entrenched stances, grand or national strategies may be helpful to prescribe common ends and ways. Concurrently, their language refers to general terms that prevent open dissent and are broad enough to allow all state organizations as well as IOs and NGOs to pursue their own interests. At the very least, the capability of grand or national strategies to achieve unity of effort should not be overestimated.

This provides a significant reason for thinking critically about the concept of Grand or National Strategy. At this level of strategy, the description of ends, ways, and means remains vague. Grand Strategy requests interagency cooperation; however it is not sufficient in providing unity of effort, since the formulation of ends gives room for divergent interpretations. Indeed, it offers the opportunity to hide national or organizational interests under broad common goals.

A huge gap exists between Grand Strategy and the operational and tactical requirements. Proposals are being discussed to fill this gap by referring to a strategic approach that is more in line with Clausewitz's understanding of strategy as a "war plan". He defines strategy as "the use of the engagement for the purpose of war."[222] From this point of view, strategy should not focus so much on the ultimate end-state with all the decisive points in between. Rather, it should be focused on setting a general perspective and some initial points from which the campaign can proceed. Thus, strategy accepts the difficulties in defining clear-cut political objectives, conducts backward planning not from the ultimate but initial objectives, and maintains its adaptability to unknown future developments. As Hew Strachan argues, "Strategy occupies the space between a desired outcome, presumably shaped by the national interest, and contingency, and it directs the outcome of a battle or other major event to fit with the objectives of policy as best it can. It also recognizes that strategy may itself have to bend in response to events. Essential here is the need for flexibility and adaptability; the need for real-time and short-

---

[222] Clausewitz, *On War*, 177.

term awareness, as well as long-term perspectives, and the need to balance the opportunity costs of both."[223]

The need and strong desire for intra-governmental collaboration has led to several initiatives to overcome its integral challenges. On the operational and tactical levels, the Provincial Reconstruction Teams (PRT) in Afghanistan are the most well-known attempts. The PRT provide interesting illustrations of how the comprehensive approach is burdened by different organizational cultures, interests, and fears that their own agency might lose its independency. As a result of the dominance of the military, other agencies place high emphasis on defending their independence. In particular, they do not want to be incorporated into the military's rigid command and control system. This appears to be a justified objective. However, when this objective hinders collaboration but instead increases fears and reduces adaptability, it becomes counter-productive.

Challenges in collaboration may cause deep frustrations among all involved. In fact, the military is more affected by these frustrations due to a variety of reasons:

1)   While military leaders of all levels traditionally pursue military victory, politicians need to have a broader approach. Seeking only victory would degrade their responsibility as "intelligent faculty". They know that victory for its own sake can lead to endless war, and thus to the deprivation of policy. If politicians question the goal of victory, military personnel may regard this as an attack on their profession and their morale.

2)   Policy expects the military to withdraw as soon as possible from their areas of operations. Military commanders, therefore, act under time pressure. Often, they are expected to provide short-term results. By contrast, diplomats and development agents typically remain after the termination of the violent conflict.

3)   Political leaders or leaders of civil organizations may shy away from delivering clear political objectives or from be-

---

[223] Strachan, Hew, "Strategy and Contingency", *International Affairs* 87:6 (2011), 1295. See also Lindley, Nick, "Redpointing' Strategy: A Model for Strategy-making in Contemporary Conflict", *Royal College of Defence Studies*, July 2013.

ing linked to how the military uses its instruments to achieve the desired political results. This may give them a chance of being perceived as not responsible for the outcome and enable them to blame the military commander.

4) Military leaders possess a strong can-do mentality including the willingness to take risks. They want to achieve decisive results as soon as possible, they push for actions in situations characterized by uncertainty, and they favor independent action. By contrast, civil leaders appear more reflective, risk averse and dependent on guidance from their respective ministries/agencies.

5) Due to the nature of warfare, the military conducts a decision-making process precisely scheduled by a battle rhythm that requires significant planning capabilities. Civil partners usually do not possess the quantity and quality of personnel to contribute fully to the different staff processes. Freedom of action may also be more restrained. Civil ministries often do not delegate decisions to the operational level as is done within the military's mission command leadership philosophy. Protecting their independence from the overwhelming dominance of the military in mission areas, representatives of civil ministries and organizations may deliberately refrain from getting too much involved in operational planning processes. They must prevent by all means their becoming subordinated to the military or to committing too many resources to achieving military objectives.

6) Military operations usually last several weeks or months. Often, they are planned and executed on short notice. By contrast, projects sponsored and managed by diplomats and development agents are often long-term projects with durations of many years. Consequently, the planning horizons are different. Even if civil partners agree to contribute to military operations, means often cannot be made available at short notice.

7) Military personnel changes more often than civilian personnel. New leaders typically appear with new proposals, projects and procedures. These may not always be appre-

ciated by the civil personnel that may see military personnel as coming and going without providing longlasting contributions.

8)   Political decisions on national security issues are often highly influenced by domestic politics. From the military's point of view, it may appear as if the political leaders are not fully committed to the war efforts. At some point, generals also may become concerned about domestic politics, when they recognize the need for improved strategic communication to enhance the support of the "home front". If politicians are reluctant or not capable of maintaining public support, the military may step in, thus intruding on the realm of domestic politics. The U.S. military appears to be highly inclined towards this course of action, due to a high reputation within society. Politicians may be suspicious of any hidden agenda pursued by famous military leaders.[224]

9)   Last but not least, and probably most importantly, stability operations require "political generals", as Hew Strachan argues. "'Political' is used here in a non-partisan and entirely unpejorative sense: it just means that officers have to be able to negotiate as well as to fight, to be sensitive to others' culture as well as to the morale of their own units."[225]. Although this appears to be common sense, the military leaders' political actions may increase tensions with senior civil leaders of the home nation as well as of the host nation.

These frustrations can disturb and disrupt civil-military relations, as the example of General McChrystal during his command in Afghanistan demonstrates. As Hew Strachan explains, McChrystal's

---

[224] During the Kosovo War, then SACEUR General Wesley A. Clark was expected to run for presidency in the U.S. Strategist Bernard Brodie cautions: "When they (military commanders) win with great national acclaim they tend to become high risks, possibly difficult to control and certainly difficult to replace." (Brodie, *War and Politics,* 79). See also Cohen, *Supreme Command,* 215-218.
[225] Strachan, *The Direction of War,* 219.

dismissal in June 2010 was precipitated less by his disregard of the primacy of policy or by his attempt at a military conspiracy than by the fact that he and his staff were deeply frustrated about the performance of their civil partners in supporting the agreed-upon COIN operational strategy.[226] Considering that his political guidance is unclear, variable, and too broad to be deliverable in strategic terms, General McChrystal might also have been frustrated by his Commander-in-Chief, U.S. President Barack Obama.[227]

In general, the decision-making processes in national capitals are a good source of friction in civil-military cooperation. In developing strategies, distrust can disturb the cooperation at the highest level of leadership, as former Secretary of Defense, Robert Gates, describes in his memoir: "I was aware of Biden's (U.S. Vice President who played a major role in the elaboration of a new strategy for Afghanistan and Pakistan in 2009; U.H.) conviction–and probably that of others in the room–that this request (for more troops; U.H.) and the McChrystal assessment (on the situation in Afghanistan; U.H.) were part of an orchestrated squeeze play by the military to get the president to approve a lot more troops. I described my own reservations about a big increase in troop numbers but didn't see why two or four thousand more troops should cause so much *angst and hostility* (highlighted by me; U.H.)."[228]

The main critique addressed towards the responsible political leaders is their real or perceived lack of understanding. As General Sir Rupert Smith argues, "the politicians quite rightly expect the military to respond to their requirements, but too often do so without any comprehension of the practical considerations of the matter, let

---

[226] *Ibid.*, 210-211; see also Gates, *Duty*, 487-489. This was different in the case of General MacArthur. As Bernard Brodie argues, "he was dismissed ... not for his differences [with President Truman] but for his insubordination in repeatedly making them public in a manner clearly designed to exert pressure upon the President." (Brodie, *War and Politics*, 58; see also 81-91).

[227] Paul Kan discusses how the withdrawal from Afghanistan puts stress on the civil-military relations. The military can be expected to blame the politicians for not having the will to fight until victory is achieved, while politicians are frustrated with the military because they do not win in spite of all resources made available to them. See Kan, "Making a Sandwich in Afghanistan," 6-7.

[228] Gates, *Duty*, 349.

alone conceptual ones. If force is to continue to be used, and to have utility, this situation must change".[229]

When the political leaders and their staffs are unfamiliar with the nature of war as well as with military culture[230], when they shy away from taking over responsibility for military actions, when they are suspicious of the political motives of the senior military leaders, when they lack confidence in their commanders in the field and even in any part of the strategy, and thus, as a consequence, their civilian staff attempts to micromanage military operations by directly intervening at operational headquarters, then the quality of the civil-military relations will drastically deteriorate.[231]

Frustrations of the military can be fuelled when the personnel strength of the civil agencies and their contributions to achieve the political objectives are well below expectations. The civilian surge in Afghanistan, although clearly laid down in the directive dated 19 November 2009[232], remained at a low level. Gates stresses his and also the tactical commanders' frustrations when he writes in his memoirs: "I was concerned that a high percentage of the U.S. civilians in Afghanistan were stationed in Kabul, when the greatest need was in the provinces and districts where our military was attempting to clean out the Taliban. They stayed a year—with a number of weeks of vacation time—and nearly all turned over in the summer, often leaving gaps in civilian capability for months and sometimes indefinitely. The numbers and location of civilian experts would remain a source of frustration among our commanders and the rest of us at Defense."[233] If underperformance is linked with conflicting personalities on both the civilian and the military sides, if different policies and assessments exist, resulting in the civil side's attempts to influence the military's operational and tactical levels through direct intervention, while military leaders act more independently in the political realm, consequentially, cooperation will not only be disrupted but, in fact, "poisoned".

---

[229] Smith, *The Utility of Force*, xiv.

[230] Gates, *Duty*, 589; see also Brodie, *War and Politics*, 7.

[231] Gates, *Duty*, 363-364, 488.

[232] See here Annex 2.

[233] Gates, *Duty*, 348.

Friction also occurs during the implementation of strategies. Again, the new U.S. strategy for Afghanistan may serve as an example:

- Previous U.S. Ambassador to Afghanistan and former Lieutenant General Karl Eikenberry did not fully support the COIN approach since he believed that this operational strategy would fail due to the deficiencies of the Kabul government.[234]

- Diplomats and development agents at the regional and local levels were not willing to or capable of supporting McChrystal's "government in a box" approach. Fred Kaplan describes the concept as follows: "an enormous apparatus–more than a thousand police, a new governor, and vast teams of administrators, all Afghans-standing by, all set to swoop into Marja (a district in Helmand province) the moment the shooting was over and the insurgents were cleared. As the tens of thousands of America's surge troops began to arrive in country, the process would start up again in another town, then another, all along the Helmand River, out to the edge of the border with Pakistan. At that point, he predicted, a critical mass of Taliban leaders would abandon their hopes for victory and seek a political settlement, which would soon spark the end of the war".[235] However, the operational reality would prove to be entirely different from these aspirations. The troops could not secure the area and hand it over to the Afghan police; administrators vanished away when they realized that the district was still too dangerous to police and govern; the Afghan president torpedoed the approach due to his interests in supporting sectarian groups only; and the Ambassador Eikenberry continued to support large infrastructure projects.[236]

The military also has ample opportunity to spoil civil-military relations, in particular, when leaders too often deliver public state-

---

[234] Gates, *Duty*, 371, 380.
[235] Kaplan, *The Insurgents*, 330; see also Gates, *Duty*, 485.
[236] *Ibid.*, 330-339.

ments or leak documents.[237] Thus, they appear to undermine the supremacy of policy and provoke the belief, in particular among the responsible politicians and their personal staffs, of the political leaders being boxed in or of insubordination, revolt, and even a military coup.[238] In fact, through uncoordinated public statements, the military may truly narrow the freedom of action of their political superiors. This, in return, may force the latter to harsh reactions in order to demonstrate publicly to their constituencies that they are still in control of the military.

To some extent, strategy making is always influenced by domestic political considerations. In actuality, if democratically elected political leaders wage wars, they have to balance war efforts with domestic issues. The more war is limited, the less efforts politicians will devote to war making. This has a direct impact on the formulation and implementation of strategy: Military leaders may believe that their political masters do not fully commit themselves to the war effort; they may even sense that the latter are not convinced of the agreed upon strategy. If they are unsure where their superiors stand and consequently start putting pressure on them to reinforce their commitment, military leaders will likely fall into the trap of self-fulfilling prophecies. The U.S. strategy making for Afghanistan in 2009 resulted, as Robert Gates describes it, in a "divided house" and a "team of rivals".[239] This situation gave birth to friction and frustration. Those who suffered most from its strategic consequences are the military and the civil personnel operating in harm's way.

Senior military leaders feel justified in demanding clear political objectives from their political superiors that can be transferred to operational goals. In reality, political leaders are often unable to provide such clarifications. Instead, they may only refer to abstract aspirations and ask for the development of strategic options (that include political objectives). Military leaders should understand that politicians often face the same intellectual challenges as commanders in the field: They are confronted with uncertainty and information overload, with the burden of responsibility and the threat of losing

---

[237] *Ibid.*, 367; Brodie, *War and Politics,* 58.
[238] *Ibid.*, 378.
[239] *Ibid.*, 385.

(in their case: popular support or elections). In accordance with Clausewitz, one may describe it as a kind of "fog of politics". Like warfare, politics is an "action in a resistant element."[240] The German sociologist Max Weber describes policy as "drilling thick pieces of wood", for which leaders need to have three qualities: passion, a feeling of responsibility, and a sense of proportion.[241] This characterization may help lead to a better understanding of why strategy making, in particular the elaboration of political objectives that are translatable into operational actions, is so difficult. Military leaders should be aware of these limitations in the political realm. In the end, one may argue that war as continuation of policies and politics implies that political and military leaders need the same intellectual and moral capabilities and virtues. The awareness of sitting in the same boat should not only facilitate cooperation but defy politicians to interrogate their commanders and military advisors, and expect definite answers. At the same time, the military should be willing and capable to address critical questions to their political bosses.

The analysis of the different sources for friction raises the question of how to overcome it. While several scholars have demanded that senior military leaders educate politicians,[242] the arguments developed in this book instead seek to emphasize a reciprocal process of learning from each other. Partnership on an equal level, together with discourse-style communication, is the most effective way to improve civil-military relations. Part of this enterprise must be the clarification of assumptions and expectations on both sides. Civil-military relations should be established on the basis of constructive criticism, not on formal subordination.[243]

---

[240] Clausewitz, *On War*, 120.

[241] John Patrick Diggins, *Max Weber. Politics and the Spirit of Tragedy*, New York (Basic Books 1996), 256-257.

[242] Smith, *The Utility of War*, 326. By contrast, Cohen appears to rather encourage political leaders to educate generals. See Cohen, *Supreme Command*, 50.

[243] Kotter, *Leading Change*, 102. In fact, the discourse on strategies should strive to become an ideal speech situation, as developed by the German philosopher Jürgen Habermas, and as incorporated into the constructivist theory of international relations by Thomas Risse, „Let's argue!: Communicative Action in World Politics", *International Organization*, 54, 1, Winter 2000, 10. Several examples exist on communicative styles that do not meet the requirements of strategy making. U.S. President Lyndon Johnson's communication is analyzed in H. R. McMaster, *Dereliction of*

In spite of Robert Gates' statement that "the relationship between senior military leaders and the civilian commander in chief–the president–is often a tense one"[244]–history also provides some examples of more smooth civil-military cooperation at the highest level of leadership, such as between President Roosevelt and his Chief of Army Staff, General Marshall, during World War II.[245] Reasons for this fruitful cooperation included not only the personalities of both but also General Marshall's behavior. As biographer Mark Stoler argues, Marshall was an "apolitical soldier", in addition to being "a servant and defender of but not a participant in civilian society and its partisan politics".[246] Marshall understood his profession in such a way that he gave purely military advice to his political superiors. He was aware of the political consequences of military action, but he "refused to … attempt to make political decisions or even to give political advice, on the ground that this would be a usurpation of presidential prerogatives."[247] Being apolitical, however, did not prevent Marshall from defending his professional assessments in his conversations with President Roosevelt or allied strategic leaders such as Winston Churchill; indeed, Roosevelt expected him to do so. Being apolitical also did not exclude him from successful cooperation with the U.S. Congress and media. As Stoler argues, Marshall's apolitical stance facilitated the establishment of trustful relations with these two institutions that were tasked with controlling the military and also the president.

Duty. Lyndon Johnson, Robert McNamara, the Joint Chiefs of Staff, and the Lies that Led to Vietnam, New York (Harper Perennial) 1998, 110, 116, 131; Larry Berman, *Planning a Tragedy. The Americanization of the War in Vietnam*, New York (Norton) 1982, 82, 89, 94-99, 112-121, 126. Johnson often tried to forge consensus between his advisors that prevented controversial discussions and critical analysis. Eliot Cohen describes Donald Rumsfeld's „style of questioning" and Winston Churchill's „art of interrogation" in *Supreme Command*, 239-240 and 118-132.

[244] *Ibid.*, 573.

[245] Another historical example is the relationship between Winston Churchill and Charles Portal, Chief of the Air Staff. See Tami Davis Biddle, "Portal and Churchill: Their Wartime Relationship, 1942-1945", *Air Power Leadership: Theory and Practice*, London (The Stationary Office) 2002, 178-198.

[246] Stoler, Mark A., *George C. Marshall. Soldier-Statesman of the American Century*, Detroit (Twayne Publishers) 1989, 23.

[247] *Ibid.*, 126.

Due to the modern challenges of security policy and strategy making, however, generals should raise the political implications of strategic options as well as the political prerequisites for military success in their interactions with politicians. Marshall became a role model for the apolitical military culture; this role model was intellectually reinforced by Huntington's concept of the professional soldier in the nuclear age. In modern "wars amongst the people", it is questionable if this apolitical attitude is possible or advisable. The apolitical stance that attempts to remain purely professional belongs to the old paradigm of industrial war and does not fit into most of the new security challenges. The relevance of information requires political and military leaders to coordinate clearly who is to deliver which political messages. Excluding the military from interaction with the people gives clear evidence that civil-military relations are tense. Military leaders should think more in term of politics (and not primarily policies). It is important to recognize that Clausewitz defined war as continuation of policies *and politics*. Only if military leaders are capable of giving advice from the perspective of the responsible political leaders, can political objectives and military action be linked. Both, the politicians as well as the military, have to draw conclusions from this.[248]

Another situation of disrupted civil-military cooperation is between the government of the host nation on the one side and the civil and military leaders of the intervention states on the other. Again, as Gates stresses, Afghanistan may serve as an example of the negative impact possible if these relations are disturbed.[249] The tensions between the U.S. officials, such as Richard Holbrooke and Karl Eikenberry, and the Afghan president also contributed to the operational challenges General McChrystal faced. In reality, if the government of the host nations is highly criticized, its actions may be regarded as strategically irrelevant. This attitude might have caused the misunderstanding of reintegration as a COIN tool only, not as an overarching political initiative. It appears that a "divided house" on the side of the invention states is not helpful in understanding and supporting the policies of the host nation.

---

[248] Smith, *The Utility of Force*, 309.
[249] Gates, *Duty*, 348, 484, 489.

Overall, friction, frustration, and fights between the U.S. civil and military stakeholders in the development of the new strategy in 2009 caused some paradoxes. The not fully fledged COIN approach that was blended with elements of Counter Terrorism, put under significant time pressure due to the announced withdrawal of troops, and challenged by divergent assessments about the political and military situation in Afghanistan, particularly with respect to the government of President Karsai, was not designed for success. In addition, the potential of the APRP was not fully understood and utilized. The new U.S. strategy for Afghanistan is an example of how flaws in the development of one's own strategies not only affect operational or tactical successes but also major political initiatives of the host nation.

If the policies and strategies of the different stakeholders are not aligned, improvements in the education of those who are expected to cooperate will probably remain insufficient. Even if the partners are well aware of the cultural differences among the various organizations, cooperation will remain a constant challenge. Clausewitz's insight that the logic may be the same but not the grammar remains valid. Differences are determined by the 'nature' of the various subjects. They will be increased by divergent policies. They can hardly be overcome at the operational and tactical levels– neither by the best efforts of individuals involved, nor by initiatives "to build understanding and synchronize plans" or organizational improvements[250].

What are the implications of this analysis for reintegration? Reintegration is an approach to peace and security that goes beyond organizational silos and boundaries. Reintegration has a security, diplomatic, intelligence, development, and justice dimension. This places significant challenges on the host nation in executing the programs. International support is therefore necessary. This support should not be provided by the military but through a whole-of-government approach, with the civil partners in the lead. If it comes to administrative shortfalls, it is less the military's responsibility to

---

[250] US Department of State, *3D Planning Guide*, July 2012; Raymond A. Millen, Carolyn Pruitt, "The Government Assistance Center: A Vehicle for Transitioning to the Host Government", *PKSOI Papers*, Carlisle, May 2011.

support with personnel but rather that of other agencies. Political pressure to overcome administrative shortfalls or political motivated obstructions should not only be executed through Key Leader Engagement by military leaders but also through civilian channels. Civil experts (and not so much military personnel) should be made available to advise the responsible officials of the host nation in the administration of the program. Medium- and long-term economic projects should be launched in districts and communities with a significant amount of reintegrated former combatants who search for job opportunities. Military Quick Impact Projects are not sufficient. Development projects in rural areas realized through reintegration programs should be linked with other, often larger, development projects of the IC. NGO should be approached and involved in grievance resolution activities. Too often, the military due to the readiness of its personnel body serves as an expedient to fill gaps in areas of civil responsibility.

In Afghanistan, the U.S. was prepared to fix problems in the execution of the APRP. The need to support was already foreseen in the new U.S. strategy and incorporated in President Obama's strategic guidance. It contains the task to "improve coordination" of the Afghan-led reintegration.[251] This task is placed under the paragraph of "civilian assistance", however, in reality, the main support for the Afghan authorities was provided by the U.S. military, particularly through the Afghan Hands program.

In truth, reintegration is an ideal field, in which to practice and improve the whole-of-government and comprehensive approach in mission areas. The high potential of reintegration in the midst of a war should encourage the civil and military leaders to achieve unity of effort in their supportive actions. Considering the facts, it is reasonable to argue that the coordination and cooperation between military and civil partners in shaping an environment that supports reintegration progress is easier to conduct than in planning and executeing purely military operations.

In the end, the insight should prevail that, in spite of the diverse natures of the instruments and the different policies and cultures of the involved organizations, progress in cooperation and col-

---

[251] Woodward, *Obama's Wars*, 386-387.

laboration helps deescalating conflicts. The better the instruments of power are aligned, the less the military will have to fight.

7   Conclusion

This book is an attempt to understand reintegration as a political initiative in the midst of a war. It provides practical lessons learned from various countries throughout recent history and a theoretical analysis through the lens of strategic thought. Both perspectives offer insights that help provide a better understanding of reintegration, in order to improve the development and implementation of future reintegration programs, and to adapt the existing strategies and operational designs to meet the political objectives of reintegration.

The main reasons for the relatively successful implementation of the APRP have been the Afghan ownership, the Afghan culture, and the Afghan people who broadly support this program. However, Afghanistan will be facing the challenges of reintegration for many years to come; this requires not only a long-term international political and financial commitment, but also the consistent political will of the Afghan government, the continuous improvement of administrative capacities and capabilities, substantial support provided by the security institutions (the ANSF as well as ISAF and, eventually, its successor organization), and the enduring commitment of the people to live together with potentially dissatisfied former combatants.

Seen through the lens of strategic thought, the definition of war as continuation of policies and politics clearly prescribes that the military does not only have to understand and support reintegration but also to adjust its ends, ways, and means in order to align them with the political purposes of reintegration. Theory and practice stress that reintegration in war relies on the availability and the credible (threat of) use of military force. Nonetheless, its utility must be adapted to the ends, ways, and means of reintegration.

The definition of war as a "paradoxical trinity" helps to understand reintegration as multilayered interaction. The discourse among the government, the military, and the people takes place within and between nations involved in a conflict. It is a very complex, adaptive and, often, contradictory system, in which the roles of the people in implementing social reintegration and of the military commander in creatively supporting reintegration progress are of utmost importance.

The integral linkage of reintegration with the envisioned peace decreases the importance of military victory that had formerly been at the center of military strategic thought. In actuality, substitutes for victory do exist. Reintegration with its focus on the underlying causes of conflicts and on conflict resolution at all levels of the host nation can help achieve tactical successes in fighting insurgents, in holding terrain, and in building up local security forces to generate a strategic outcome. Coordination with the utility of other instruments of power is also essential–for the reintegration progress as well as for military success. Furthermore, reintegration contributes to challenging critically one's own political and cultural assumptions and biases; it is the recognition that neither the host nation nor the intervening nations can kill their way to victory.

Cultural predispositions in the development and implementation of strategies may be supportive of reintegration, but can also emerge as obstacles. The people as well as the military personnel of the troop contributing nations may find it even more difficult to understand and support reintegration than the people and the military of the host country. However, the opposite can also be true.

With respect to future security challenges, reintegration reinforces the need for the whole-of-government and the comprehensive approach; however, it puts even more stress on the execution of these complicated ways of solving complex security challenges. It also encourages the establishment of a human war fighting function but places still greater emphasis on linking all military actions to the envisioned peace (and not so much on defeating the enemy or winning battles).

The theories of limited wars underline the need and the potential for reintegration. COIN as an operational strategy may become more effective in terms of strategic outcome if subordinated to reintegration efforts. Thus, reintegration is one of the ways to ease the burden of stability operations that are deemed less preferable by western states due to costs of time, money, and blood. At the same time the concept of reintegration will probably continue to challenge these states in the future, at least financially.

After more than a decade of war and stability operations, many western countries seem deliberately to shy away from these kinds of operations. In the U.S. National Security Strategy published in 2012, it is clearly stated: *"US forces will no longer be sized to conduct large-scale, prolonged stability operations"*. Emphasizing the use of non-military means, the U.S. national strategy supports the main conclusion of this book to evaluate carefully the feasibility, acceptability, and suitability of reintegration programs simultaneously with the development of an operational approach for a theatre. Again, as previously noted, reintegration should not be seen merely as an essential element of COIN. In contrast, reintegration is a strategy with clearly expressed political objectives. It is not dependent on COIN that is, by contrast, a more tactical method. Most importantly, reintegration eases the burden of COIN, and of fighting in general. As scholar Raymond Millen argues, "Counterinsurgencies are protracted, but they need not be ruinous in terms of blood and treasure."[252]

Several studies indicate that stability operations comprising COIN may again become necessary. Based on his analysis of strategic cultures, retired Army Brigadier General Russell J. Howard argues that China, Iran, North Korea, and Al Qaeda "increase their propensity for use of terrorist and guerrilla tactics … as part of a threatening rhetoric of ambiguity and unpredictability. All four should be expected to use asymmetric warfare against the United States. Therefore, U.S. policymakers must strengthen the country's primary counter-asymmetric warfare forces and organization".[253] Analyst Nathan Freier and his team from the CSIS International Security Program have come to similar conclusions. Focusing on potential disorder threats, they identify several future war fighting scenarios. The most demanding operations would be those with complex hybrid or irregular threats in a failed or failing state with substantial CBRN capabilities. As possible scenarios, the authors name Syria and Yemen, or a collapse of Pakistan, civil wars in Egypt, Saudi-Arabia, and a failing North Korea. The proper response to these scenarios would be the strategy of "distributed security". It "combines combat

---

[252] Millen, "Time for a Strategic and Intellectual Pause in Afghanistan", 43; see also Kaplan, *The Insurgents,* 354-366. However, as Paul Kan argues, there are no happy withdrawals. (Kan, "Making a Sandwich in Afghanistan", 12).
[253] Howard, *Strategic Culture*, 86.

and security tasks and is concerned with gaining control over and securing geography, infrastructure, populations, or dangerous military capabilities threatened by foreign disorder."[254]

With respect to military means, the authors underline that high-tech and stand-off means are not truly effective. Disorder scenarios are conflicts amongst the people. Potential opponents such as China and Iran are not so non-intelligent to risk conventional war against the superior U.S. armed forces. States who intend to change the order to their advantage will likely take an indirect approach by using the people in order to create disorder first. If possible, they will focus on radicalizing those people who are opposing the U.S. or the entirety of Western civilization. This is a more intelligent approach because the U.S. cannot take advantage of its military superiority, if the people are involved.[255] Even a war with North Korea would be hybrid in character from the beginning. Consequently, Freier and his team propose that combat remains the core competency but also that distributed security should be the target for optimization. This strategy can be built upon experiences from Iraq and Afghanistan. Also strategist Max Boot makes a strong argument for terrorism and insurgencies as the dominant forms of warfare in the future.[256]

These studies indicate that the strategic relevance of the people within Clausewitz's paradoxical trinity has changed. This is the case not only for the populace of democratic states that have a vote in the development of strategies, but also for the people living in war zones. Due to the decreasing capabilities of states to govern the people (governance gap), the utility of social networks not only to influence people but also to coordinate their actions, and also the availability of disruptive technology for groups or even individuals, the people have been significantly empowered, often at the expense of the government as well as of the military. Therefore, the traditional image of the state as a rational actor and functioning unit should be counterbalanced by seeing it "as an organized collection of citizens

---

[254] Freier, Nathan, "Beyond the Last War. Balancing Ground Forces and Future Challenges Risk in USCENTCOM and USPACOM", *A Report of the CSIS International Security Program*, April 2013, IX.

[255] Smith, *The Utility of Force*, 411.

[256] Howard, *Strategic Culture*, 86; Freier, "Beyond the Last War", 60; Boot, *Invisible Armies*, XX.

with highly individuated private interests", as U.S.-strategist Bernard Brodie previously stressed at the end of the Vietnam War in 1973, and British General Sir Rupert Smith further developed this concept of "war amongst the people".[257] If states are failing or have already failed, the relevance of the people becomes even more significant. In these cases, as Smith argues, "the nation-state is fighting for its supremacy".[258] Often, such a struggle will fail, at least in the medium or long term.

The new paradigm of "war amongst the people" stresses, as Rupert Smith argues, "the people amongst whom the fight will take place. We have seen that the trend of being amongst the people can have two manifestations: the presence of the fighting amongst the people and the appearance of the forces and the fighting to the people, both those amongst whom it takes place and those informed by the media."[259] In addition, as the insurgency in Afghanistan exemplifies, the people may also take an active part in the fighting – as young men are coerced to fight due to hedging behaviour or economic reasons, or as specific groups or large crowds are utilized to conduct violent actions to destabilize a state, to force the intervention forces to cause collateral damage, or to justify external political and military interference. If the utility of one's own forces is limited, the involvement of the people or of subgroups in the crisis or war areas is useful to pursue political objectives. Foreign military forces, in particular, are unlikely to engage in conflict against the people of the host nation. Opposing political and military leaders will exploit all opportunities to operate "below the threshold of the utility of our weapon systems,"[260] particularly when these are superior to any other armed forces.

The relevance of people is manifested, as well, in the fact that many opponent groups do not have formed or formal armed forces. They are, rather, a network that may be embedded within the people in diverse ways.[261]

---

[257] Brodie, *War and Politics*, 3; Smith, *The Utility of Force*.
[258] Smith, *The Utility of Force*, 307.
[259] *Ibid.*, 320.
[260] *Ibid.*, 330.
[261] *Ibid.*, 331-334.

The overall challenge remains: How can military forces optimize the utility of force in such a way that it tackles the root causes of conflict while at the same time closely cooperating with civil partners, having no clear-cut political objectives, and knowing that these objectives will, quite often, emerge only during the course of the conflict management?

This assessment of future security challenges supports the main proposition of this book that reintegration should be a major element of the development of strategies: in comparison with battles, reintegration has a higher potential to stabilize critical areas, and to create conditions for peace not so greatly burdened by grievances that they make the resumption of violence likely. It is more in line with Just War prescriptions as a basis for legitimizing military interventions, and with the avoidance of casualties and costs, although it may be not compatible with the prevailing strategic culture. Consequently, reintegration should not start at the end of a conflict fought with military means but be considered at the beginning of a conflict or even before, during contingency planning.

Reintegration may not be a suitable way for all future conflicts. Nontheless, at the start of any development of strategies, reintegration should be assessed in its suitability, feasibility, and acceptance to achieve the political objectives. Reintegration and reconciliation should also have an impact on the force structures, doctrines, and professional education systems of the armed forces of the host nation as well as on the intervention nations[262]. As Bob Woodward suggests, President Obama, the National Security Adviser, James L. Jones, and the Chief of the Joint Chiefs of Staff, Admiral Mullen realized the linkage between reintegration and the drawdown of coalition forces during the process of developing a new strategy for Afghanistan. Therefore, the organization of military staffs as well as the education of leaders at all levels must take reintegration as a potential element of strategy into account.

The military must strive for a better understanding and support the desired outcome of reintegration. Several opportunities do exist. Consequently, reintegration is a field in which the military can demonstrate its utility in achieving a political outcome. Nevertheless,

---

[262] Woodward, *Obama's Wars*, 229-230, 269.

one must be aware that this cannot be achieved by the military alone, and the military can only be a support. The successes of tactical action in securing communities that have inserted former combatants or in putting pressure on low- and mid-level commanders must be exploited by civilian organizations of the host nation as well as the IC in order to generate a strategic outcome. If a military operation is understood within the paradigm of "war amongst the people", reintegration of opponent fighters comes to the fore.

Reintegration cannot replace the use or threat of violence. The capabilities of the national security and the intervention forces to fight successfully, as well as its perception by the people have a decisive influence on the insurgent's willingness to reintegrate. If reintegration is pursued, military operations have to be adapted not only to support reintegration (and reconciliation) efforts to the greatest extent possible but also be more thoroughly equipped to meet the overall political purpose: a better sustained peace, not necessarily a decisive victory.

Reintegration also stresses the need for civil-military relations that are optimized to the development of strategies–not only in the execution of reintegration and its supportive measures but also in linking political objectives with the operational and tactical conduct of war. Civil-military relations have a tendency to become tenser during the course of a war. When it comes to the development of strategies, they must be nested in a discourse on an equal level, not in subordination of the military or in separation of responsibilities. As Hew Strachan concludes, "Strategy will not flourish if the armed services are silent on the issue, or feel themselves to be constrained by norms in relation to the proper and 'politically correct' conduct of civil-military relations."[263] Political leaders need to facilitate this new professionalism.

Interacting with their political masters, generals and admirals should raise the political implications of strategic options as well as the political prerequisites for military success. General Marshall became a role model for the apolitical military culture. In modern "wars amongst the people", this apolitical attitude is not possible or advisable. The apolitical stance that attempts to remain purely professional

---

[263] Strachan, *The Direction of War*, 25.

belongs to the old paradigm of industrial war and does not fit into most of the new security challenges. Stability operations make military commanders more political, since they get involved in state and nation building.[264] Military leaders should think more in term of politics (and not only policies) to better understand the constraints of limited wars. Only if military leaders are capable of giving advice from the perspective and context of the responsible political leaders, can political objectives and military action be linked. Evidently, military leaders have to conduct tasks that bring them more in conflict with civil partners than ever before.[265]

---

[264] Hew Strachan detected the politization of the military engaged in colonial warfare. See Hew Strachan, *The Politics of the British Army*, Oxford (University Press) 1997.

[265] Strachan, *The Direction of War*, 219; Smith, *The Utility of Force*, 309.

8 Recommendations for the Military (in case the Support of Reintegration within a Host Nation is decided upon)

Political level:

- Underscore peace as the ultimate political goal of war in strategic communication with the public and in guidance given to subordinated instruments of national power.

- Adjusts the military ends, ways, and means to the political objectives of the reintegration program, if applicable.

- Contribute to improving the whole-of-government approach within the National Security System as well as in mission theatres.

Strategic level:

- Conduct the FAS[266] test of reintegration for potential conflicts in Operational Concepts and Contingency Plans.

- Shape the environment in potential conflict areas in such a way that opportunities for reintegration can be swiftly utilized.

- Direct operations and tactics to meet better the political goals of reintegration in conflict scenarios.

- Align and subordinate the concept and the implementation of COIN to the purpose of reintegration, if applicable.

- Facilitate the utility of all available instruments of national/multinational power in an overall coordinated campaign to support reintegration.

- Link the tactical results achieved by the different instruments to the overall political purpose of reintegration.

---

[266] Feasibility, Acceptability, Suitability.

- Continue to adjust the strategic culture to fulfill better the requirements of "war amongst the people" (human domain as a 7th war fighting function).

- Incorporate the purpose of reintegration and its impact on the development and adaption of strategies in professional military education.

- Further improve the interagency cooperation by utilizing the support of reintegration as a common effort.

- Educate personnel with specific cultural expertise that are also capable of supporting host nations in the conceptualization and implementation of reintegration programs.

Operational and tactical level:

- Adapt staff structures in operational and tactical headquarters to improve the support of civil partners.

- Incorporate reintegration in operational planning (operational art, operational design, and any planning processes).

- Conduct military operations (particularly Information Operations and Special Operations) designed to shape the environment for reintegration progress.

Appendix:

Carl von Clausewitz's Relevance for Strategic Thought

Clausewitz's theory of war offers the most comprehensive intellectual approach to comprehending national security challenges. This appendix argues that strategic thinkers such as Basil Liddell Hart who placed critiques of Clausewitz at the center of his scholarly writings often misunderstood the main propositions of the Prussian general. In reality, their alternative propositions such as the indirect approach are limited in explanatory power and can be easily incorporated into Clausewitz's theory of war. Furthermore, the new security threats imposed by non-state actors do not falsify Clausewitz's main propositions. By contrast, his theoretical insights shed light also on the use of violence by terrorist or insurgent groups. In addition, Clausewitz's theory best captures the increased role that politicians have assumed in the making of military strategy. Finally, the supreme explanatory power of Clausewitz's theory of war relies on its design: With its dialectical structure, its confrontation of theoretical insights with experience, its self-limitation with respect to prescriptions, and the central role attributed to the responsible individual, Clausewitz's theory is highly suitable to understand and cope with complex security environments. His methodological approach serves as a role model of how to reflect on security challenges in order to grasp their ceaseless changing character and thereby respecting the fundamental nature of conflict. Consequently, Clausewitz offers a paradigm to strategic thinking that can be the basis for intra-governmental, as well as, for multinational cooperation within alliances.

The intellectual Shortfalls of those who love to criticize Clausewitz

Carl von Clausewitz[1] foresaw that his opus magnum would inspire strong criticism.[2] Basil Liddell Hart[3] was one of the main critics of Clausewitz. Not only did he disqualify Clausewitz's writings as "obscure" and "outdated"[4] but also blamed him for preaching unlimited war and accused him of being responsible for the manslaughter of World War I[5]. Reflecting upon his experience in the Great War, Liddell Hart developed the *indirect approach*[6] as the main principle of achieving strategic success. However, the British strategist's intellectual approach suffers from shortcomings. Instead of trying to understand Clausewitz comprehensively, he based his critiques primarily on how the German General Staff misunderstood the Prussian phi-

---

[1] For biographical information about Carl von Clausewitz, see Peter Paret, *Clausewitz and the State*, Princeton/New Jersey (Princeton University Press) 1985.

[2] See Carl von Clausewitz, "Two Notes by the Author on His Plans for Revising On war," *On War*, edited and translated by Michael Howard and Peter Paret, Princeton/New Jersey (Princeton University Press) 1984: 70. Werner Hahlweg, Germany's primary Clausewitz expert, described the reception of Clausewitz's *On War* in his article "Das Clausewitzbild einst und jetzt", published as a pre-text in the 19th/20th edition of *On War*, Bonn (Duemmler) 1991, 3-172.

[3] Basil Liddell Hart (1895-1970) is the most important British strategist. He served in World War I; his scholarly writings are highly influenced by the experience of this war.

[4] Liddell Hart's arguments against Clausewitz were often driven by emotion. In the new edition of Sun Tzu's *The Art of War*, Liddelll Hart wrote: „Among all the military thinkers of the past, only Clausewitz is comparable (to Sun Tzu; U.H.), and even he is more ‚dated' than Sun Tzu, and in part antiquated, although he was writing more than two thousand years later." (Sun Tzu, *The Art of War*. Translated and with an Introduction by Samuel B. Griffith, Oxford University Press (London/Oxford/New York) 1971, V.

[5] See Raymond Aron, *Clausewitz: Philosopher of War*, New Jersey (Prentice-Hall, Inc., Englewood Cliffs) 1985, 233-238.

[6] Basil Liddell Hart, *Strategy*, New York (Penguin Books) 1991, 319-333. The indirect approach is analyzed in Colin S. Gray, *Modern Strategy*, Oxford (University Press) 2012, 89. The approach can be traced back to Sun Tzu's *The Art of War*, in which is stated: "Victory is the main object in war. If this is long delayed, weapons are blunted and morale depressed. When troops attack cities, their strength will be exhausted." (73). "To subdue the enemy without fighting is the acme of skill." (77)

losopher of war before World War I.[7] The British strategist even dared to offer a magic formula to solve all strategic security challenges. Clausewitz would have criticized this Jominian promise by highlighting the significance of chance and friction in war[8]. In addition, he would have underlined the limitations and prerequisites of the indirect approach, as laid down in his historical reconstruction of Napoleon's campaign in Russia.[9] Today, it has become apparent that, as Brian H. Reid puts it, "the indirect approach is not a cure-all."[10]

John Keegan and Martin van Creveld are historians who continue Liddell Hart's method of trashing Clausewitz.[11] Without going into details of their often unjustified critiques, it needs to be clearly stated that Clausewitz was no apostle of annihilation.[12] By contrast, Clausewitz recommended an even more cautious approach to war making than Jomini and Liddell Hart, since he did not offer any op-

---

[7] See Christopher Bassford, *Clausewitz in English. The Reception of Clausewitz in Britain and America, 1815-1945*, New York/Oxford (University Press) 1994, 5; Jehuda L. Wallach, "Misperceptions of Clausewitz's On War by the German Military," in Michael I. Handel (ed.), *Clausewitz and modern Strategy*, Kansas (Frank Cass) 1986: 229. Indeed, that was also recognized by Liddelll Hart himself when he writes: "As it often happens, Clausewitz's disciples carried his teaching to an extreme which their master had not intended." (Liddelll Hart, *Strategy*, 339)

[8] Jomini went so far as to state that he claimed to have revealed the secrets of success of Napoleon's warfare, even „… to the point of predicting his actions with certainty" (Aron, *Clausewitz: Philosopher of War*, 173). Also Sun Tzu was convinced that generals who follow his principals would not fail in war. See Sun Tzu, *The Art of War*, 66.

[9] Carl von Clausewitz, "The Campaign of 1812 in Russia," in Carl von Clausewitz, *Historical and political writings*, Princeton (Princeton University Press) 1992, 143; see also Clausewitz, *On War*, 92-93.

[10] Brian Holden Reid, *Studies in British Military Thought*, Lincoln (University of Nebraska Press) 1998, 179. See also Christopher Bassford, *Clausewitz in English: The Reception of Clausewitz in Britain and America, 1815-1945*, New York (Oxford University Press), 217-218. Bassford states that contemporary British officers realized that the principals of the indirect approach were not in line with their experience of colonial warfare.

[11] Christopher Bassford, *John Keegan and the Grand Tradition of Trashing Clausewitz*, available online (http://www.clausewitz.com/readings/Bassford/Keegan/) (Accessed October 23, 2013).

[12] See Christopher Bassford, *Clausewitz in English*, 63. Bassford is correct when he argues: „Clausewitz postulated no requirement for decisive battle, demanding only an awareness of the possibility."

erational or strategic formula for guaranteed success, but underlined the incalculable risks of and in war. Indeed, one may even argue that Clausewitz is nearer to Sun Tzu in his advice to refrain from war making than Jomini and Liddell Hart are. Consequently, it is important to overcome misinterpretations of Clausewitz in order to take advantage of the deep complexity of his reflections on war and to incorporate alternative approaches into his theoretical framework. This is a prerequisite for the desired consensus on a strategic theory that can establish a paradigm of thought for the national and international security systems.

Clausewitz and Asymmetric Warfare

Clausewitz's theory of war is focused on regular wars between states. The personification of the paradoxical trinity that Clausewitz placed in the center of his theory comprises the people, the commander with his army, and the government of states. He argues, „War is more than a true chameleon that slightly adapts its characteristics to the given case. As a total phenomenon its dominant tendencies always make war a paradoxical trinity—composed of primordial violence, hatred, and enmity, which are to be regarded as a blind natural force; of the play of chance and probability within which the creative spirit is free to roam; and of its element of subordination, as an instrument of policy, which makes it subject to reason alone. The first of these three aspects mainly concern the people; the second the commander and his army; the third the government."[13] In fact, states were the main actors in international relations within the Westphalian System. Nonetheless, Clausewitz was well aware of the small wars of irregular troops as well as of the insurrections of suppressed people.[14] In spite of their significance, Clausewitz was right to give primacy to regular wars between states. Until today, only states have been capable of establishing and employing large military forces. Scholars Nye

---

[13] Clausewitz, *On War*, 89.

[14] See the chapter on „The People in Arms" in Book Six of *On War*. Clausewitz intensively analyzed small wars as an element of wars, and he studied the insurrection of the Spanish people against Napoleon. He did this not only for theoretical reasons but as a potential role model for the Prussian insurrection against the French occupation.

and Welch argue that "… states normally are the only actors that wield significant armies. Some other actors are capable of organized violence on a small scale, but functioning states have an unusual capacity to wield organized violence on a massive scale". From that point of view, Clausewitz was right to place the destructive potential of the states into the heart of his theoretical work. However, Nye and Welch admit: "In failed states or states that are experiencing civil war, substate actors occasionally have this capacity".[15] This is the case when factions have the ability to take over elements of the state's resources (such as in Syria) or when insurgents are supported by a neighboring country, such as the Taliban in Afghanistan who are supported by Pakistan. In addition, non-state actors conduct asymmetric warfare as a result of their intelligent interaction with opponent states that possess unmatched armed forces.[16] Often, the objective of their fighting is to create a new state and to transform their insurgent fighters into regular forces.

The Australian scholar Sebastian Kaempf criticized the proposition of scholars such as Martin van Creveld that the era of trinitarian war is over and, therefore, Clausewitz's theory of war is irrelevant. Kaempf argues that Clausewitz's theory is still well aligned to today's realities; however, he advocates correcting Clausewitz's dictum that insurgencies and insurrections can only succeed if supported by regular armed forces.[17] He criticizes that Clausewitz "failed to see the potential of guerrilla warfare to rise from an adjunct to conventional war to a coherently independent form of warfare."[18]

---

[15] See Joseph S. Nye, Jr., David A. Welch, *Understanding Global Conflict and Cooperation. An Introduction to Theory and History*, Boston (Longman) 2011, 38. See also P. Michael Phillips, "Deconstructing Our Dark Age Future," *Parameters*, Summer 2009, 103.

[16] See also Colin S. Gray, „Irregular warfare: Guerrillas, insurgents and terrorists", in War*, Peace and International relations*, London (Routledge) 2007: 251: „Guerrilla warfare is the character of warfare waged of necessity by irregular belligerents." From the guerrilla's or insurgent's point of view, their warfare is not limited, as the example of the Vietcong may illustrate. Only from the U.S. perspective, the Vietnam War was fought with limited objectives.

[17] Sebastian Kaempf, „Lost through non-translation: bringing Clausewitz's writings on ‚new wars' back in", *Small Wars & Insurgencies 22*, no. 4 (October 2011), 548-573.

[18] *Ibid.*, 562.

Clausewitz might not have foreseen guerrilla warfare as conducted by Mao Zedong or Thomas Edward Laurence. However, the main elements of his theory can also be applied to these independent types of warfare: The metaphor of the duel, in which each opponent tries to compel the other to do his political will through physical force[19], is helpful also to understand asymmetric warfare. Al Qaida may serve as the most recent example. Its overall political objective is to compel the U.S. to stay out of Islamic countries, and to establish its own Islamic state[20]. Its leadership has been engaged in aligning objectives with ways and means, as documented in the "Letters from Abbottabad" of Osama Bin Ladin[21]. In addition, Clausewitz's dictum on the superiority of the defense over the offensive warfare[22] is also true for asymmetric warfare: As Kissinger wrote, "The guerrilla wins if he does not lose. The conventional army loses if it does not win".[23]

The Role of Politics and Policies

Politicians have realized that war is too serious a business to leave it to the military. Clausewitz was the first to underline the overall political character of war. His proposition on war as a continuation of policies and politics is the result not only of his personal experience in state and war making in Prussia after 1806[24] but also of his theoretical reasoning.[25]

---

[19] Clausewitz, *On War*, 75.

[20] This is the traditional state-making through war-making approach. See Charles Tilly, „How War Made States and Vice Versa," *Center for Studies of Social Change, New School for Social Research*, 1987.

[21] Combating Terrorism Center at West Point, *Letters from Abbottabad. Bin Ladin Sidelined?*, 3 May 2012 (online available: http://www2.gwu.edu) (accessed 23 October 2013).

[22] Clausewitz, *On War*, 358.

[23] Henry Kissinger, „The Vietnam Negotiations", in *Foreign Affairs 47*, 1969, 214.

[24] Clausewitz contributed to the reform of the Prussian state as the assistant to Gerhard von Scharnhorst, the head of the Military Reform Commission. For detailed information, see Gordon A. Craig, *The Politics of the Prussian Army 1640-1945*, London/New York (1955/64), 37-53; Peter Paret, *Clausewitz and the State*, 137-146.

[25] Clausewitz, *On War*, 87. The primacy of policies and politics is underlined by its prominent position in chapter one of the first book of *On War*. However, many

Clausewitz underlined that, due to the political character of war, military advice without touching the realm of policies and politics is not possible. He stresses „… that a major military development, or the plan for one, should be a matter for *purely military* opinion is unacceptable and can be damaging. Nor indeed is it sensible to summon soldiers … and ask them for *purely military advice.*"[26] This was already stated by Sun Tzu, although he requested that politicians stay out of the war-making process being conducted by the general. As a consequence, it is the general himself who has to think in terms of grand strategy, in particular with respect to the impact of warfare on the economy.

On the other side, Clausewitz left no doubt where the final responsibility for war making lies—with the politicians. When the commander carries out his mission, he has to respect the political objectives in his war plan as well as during the conduct of military operations.[27] Due to chance and friction in warfare[28] as well as changes in domestic and international policies, war plans must be adapted. Again, alignment of political ends with ways and means is necessary. Consequently, constant interaction between the government and the commander based on trustful relations is required in all phases of warfare.

From this proposition, conclusions for the national security system and the strategic culture can be drawn. With respect to military leaders, education should comprise the competencies to think outside the military box and inside the political realm, and to give

---

nations needed to learn this proposition by experience, sometimes at the expense of the prosperity of their nations.

[26] Clausewitz, *On War*, 607.

[27] Clausewitz delved deeply into policies and politics during the reform of the Prussian State. Politicians may and should trust their military personnel. However, they carry the responsibility for military action in a realm that is characterized by chance.

[28] Clausewitz, *On War*, 85: „No other human activity is so continuously or universally bound up with chance. And through the element of chance, guesswork and luck come to play a great part in war." See also Clausewitz's considerations of danger, physical exhaustion, lack of information, and friction on p. 113-121. The significant emphasis of friction is unique to Clausewitz. Sun Tzu did not consider friction, as long as the strategic advice is respected by the general.

advice from the perspective of the responsible politicians. It should also ensure that the political objectives are respected in strategy making and operational warfare[29], and to empower all individuals of the armed forces to conduct their missions in the spirit of the political objectives. Today, in the era of the "strategic corporal", these conclusions are even more relevant than they were two hundred years ago.

Clausewitz's Understanding of the Nature of War and the Consequences for the Theory of War and Strategy

Reflecting upon war, Clausewitz started with philosophical considerations. How must war develop, if war is a duel with two opponents trying to impose their will on each other? He developed the idealtyp[30] that war has the tendency to escalate to absolute war. Then, he confronted this idealtyp with experience[31], and realized that wars are quite often limited. This brought him to the conclusion that war is determined by political objectives. Consequently, as Aron argues, "it is not the initial conception of absolute war which allows the historical diversity of wars to be subsumed under a single concept, but the intrinsically political nature of war".[32] With the same method of thinking, Clausewitz concluded that morale, psychology, and character matter in war. War is a social intercourse where the belligerent with numerically superior armed forces does not necessarily win. By contrast, even inferior armed forces win wars if the political objectives are better aligned to the ways and means, if the people are more engaged, if the commanders possess a higher sense of judgment[33],

---

[29] See Aron, *Clausewitz. Philosopher of war*, 83.

[30] The idealtyp-concept was developed by the German sociologist Max Weber. See Max Weber, *Essays in Sociology*, edited by H.H. Gerth and C. Wright Mills, New York 1958.

[31] Clausewitz argues: „Analysis and observation, theory and experience must never disdain or exclude each other; on the contrary, they support each other. The propositions of this book therefore, like short spans of an arch, base their axioms on the secure foundation either of experience or the nature of war as such, and are thus adequately buttressed." (Clausewitz, *On War*, 61. See also Clausewitz's critical approach to history in *On War*, 156-174.

[32] Aron, *Clausewitz. Philosopher of War*, 81.

[33] Clausewitz, *On War*, 120.

character[34], and coup d'oeil[35] to act successfully in war as "a resistant element"[36], and if the armed forces have superior military virtues.

What does that mean for the theory of war and strategy? Theory offers some fundamental insights, such as the interaction between the elements of the fascinating trinity, or that every attack loses impetus as it progresses. However, theory cannot provide any magic formula and prescriptions on how to act. In the field of war, theories cannot explain and predict (as in science), but only help to understand war in its historic variations (as in humanities). If the theory of war intends to give prescriptions, they will probably be wrong. In contrast, Clausewitz's theory is a method of thinking that is specifically tailored to fit the nature of war; it offers a framework on how to analyze war in its ceaselessly changing characteristics, and it encourages individuals to find sensible answers to strategic questions independently. Consequently, it places utmost importance on the leaders, their education and their position within the national security system.

Sun Tzu also placed greatest emphasis on the competencies of the commander. He put even more responsibility on his shoulders than Clausewitz did, since he had the sole and entire responsibility for the war (Sun Tzu argued that generals must be unconstrained by politics). Clausewitz, by contrast, saw the responsibility more in the field of independent action, and in sensing the changes in current and future war-making. Clausewitz realised that commanders cannot rely on any laws or prescriptions of warfare, such as Sun Tzu, Jomini and Liddell Hart promised to offer. The self-limitation of theory and the importance of independent reflection by strategic leaders are the main reasons why Clausewitz's thoughts are best suited to understand and cope with future security challenges. This, actually, was Clausewitz's intent when he started to write *On War*. He knew that it was the method of thinking, not so much the content of his deliberations that would survive over time. „It is not the things we have

---

[34] Clausewitz, *On War*, 108.

[35] *Ibid.*, *On War*, 102.

[36] *Ibid.*, *On War*, 120.

thought but the manner in which we have thought them that constitutes a great contribution to theory".[37]

Conclusion

Clausewitz's theory of war is still valid due to its comprehensive understanding of the volatile, uncertain, complex and adaptable intercourse between the people, the military, and the government (on their own and their opponent's side).

Clausewitz's limitations to theory are based on his understanding of education that, in the case of commanders, means self-education: „Theory exists so that one need not start afresh each time sorting out the material and ploughing through it, but will find it ready to hand and in good order. It is meant to educate the mind of the future commander, or, more accurately, to guide him in his self-education, not to accompany him to the battlefield; just as a wise teacher guides and stimulates a young man's intellectual development, but is careful not to lead him by the hand for the rest of his life."[38] By contrast, Sun Tzu would see this as a recipe for disaster. He promises to be „able to forecast which side will be victorious and which defeated. If a general who heeds my strategy is employed he is certain to win."[39]

Clausewitz discovered the underlying and very human nature of war and conflict that does not change. Not only military but also political leaders should take advantage of this theory and its methodological approach. The faster the international system changes, the more leaders will need a framework to understand better the emerging security challenges.

---

[37] Carl von Clausewitz, *Der Feldzug in 1812 in Russland und die Befreiungskriege von 1813-1815*, Berlin o.J.: 264.
[38] Clausewitz, *On War*, 141.
[39] Sun Tzu, The Art of War, 66.

Clausewitz's theory has the potential to become the guiding paradigm for all strategy makers–in the whole-of-government[40] approach of nation states as well as in multinational cooperation within alliances.[41] Clausewitz should be, as Gray argues, "First theorist of war"[42], and, as this paper adds, of any security challenge.[43]

---

[40] The pursuit of a comprehensive approach in strategy making is a logical conclusion of Clausewitz's insights into the political character of war, the primacy of policies and politics, and the complexity of war-making.

[41] A first attempt was made be Reiner Pommerin (ed.), *Clausewitz goes global. Carl von Clausewitz in the 21st Century*, Miles-Verlag (Berlin) 2011.

[42] Gray, *Modern Strategy*, 12.

[43] However, his acceptability remains hampered by misinterpretations as well as the widespread and probably increasing desire for simplicity.

Annexes:

Annex 1: President Karzai's Inauguration Speech, November 19, 2009

(…) Honorable Guests, Dear Compatriots. With international support, Afghanistan has had many successes in the past eight years; these successes have been the result of sacrifices made by our people and the peoples of our allied countries. I do not want go over all of the successes of the last eight years. I do, however, want to state that during the last eight years, we were able to bring Afghanistan out of a situation where it did not have a responsible government and the necessary legal foundations. Today, we have a law-based state along with institutions that are at the service of the people of our country. We are proud of Afghanistan's achievements in providing its sons and daughters with access to education and health services. Today, Afghanistan enjoys an open and free media, a developing civil society, a rehabilitated economic infrastructure, a set of well-conducted monetary reforms and a budding free-market economy. Grasping the opportunity of today's august occasion, I would like to talk about Afghanistan's tomorrow. We have to learn from the mistakes and shortcomings of the past eight years. It is through this self evaluation that we can better respond to the aspirations and expectations of our people. At this point, I would like to set out the priorities that will serve as the basis for our future endeavors: 1. Peace and Reconciliation: Securing peace and an end to fighting are the most significant demands of our people. For the last thirty years, our people have offered continuous sacrifices to achieve peace. It is a recognized fact that security and peace cannot be achieved through fighting and violence. This is why the Islamic Republic of Afghanistan has placed national reconciliation at the top of its peace-building policy. We welcome and will provide necessary help to all disenchanted compatriots who are willing to return to their homes, live peacefully and accept the Constitution. We invite dissatisfied compatriots, who are not directly linked to international terrorism, to return to their homeland. We will utilize all national and international resources to put an end to war and fratricide. We will call Afghanistan's traditional Loya Jirga and make every possible effort to ensure peace in our country. At this point, I am compelled to note that His Majesty King Abdullah, Custodian of the Two Holy Mosques, has made many commendable efforts towards peace and national reconciliation in Afghanistan. We thank His Majesty, the Custodian of the Two Holy Mosques, and hope that he will continue his endeavors for this cause (...)".[1]

---

[1]http://www.afghanistan-un.org/2009/11/president-karzai%E2%80%99s-inauguration-speech/

Annex 2: President Obama's final Orders for Afghanistan Pakistan Strategy, or Terms Sheet, November 29, 2009.

MEMORANDUM FOR THE PRINCIPALS
From: National Security Adviser

This memorandum summarizes the Afghan option discussed among the principals and with the president, sending significant additional U.S. troops in early 2010 in order to degrade the Taliban and set the conditions for accelerated transition to Afghan authorities beginning in July 2011.

New implementation guidance for Afghanistan

In support of our core goal, new implementation guidance for Afghanistan follows:

United States goal in Afghanistan is do deny safe haven to al Qaeda and to deny the Taliban the ability to overthrow the Afghan government.

The strategic concept for the United States, along with our international partners and the Afghans, is to degrade the Taliban insurgency while building sufficient Afghan capacity to secure and govern their country, creating conditions for the United States to begin reducing its forces by July 2011.

- The military mission in Afghanistan will focus on six operational objectives and will be limited in scope and scale to only what is necessary to attain the U.S. goal. These objectives are:
    - Reversing the Taliban's momentum.
    - Denying the Taliban access to and control of key population and production centers and lines of communication.
    - Disrupting the Taliban in areas outside the secure area and preventing al Qaeda from gaining sanctuary in Afghanistan.
    - Degrading the Taliban to levels manageable by the Afghan National Security Forces (ANSF).

o   Increasing the size of the ANSF and leveraging the potential for local security forces so we can transition responsibility for security to the Afghan government on a timeline that will permit us to begin to decrease our troop presence by July 2011.

o   Selectively building the capacity of the Afghan government with military focused on the ministries of defense and interior.

Civilian assistance

- Our military efforts and civilian assistance will be closely coordinated.

- Given the profound problems of legitimacy and effectiveness with the Karzai government, we must focus on what is realistic. Our plan concludes the way forward in dealing with the Karzai government has four elements: Working with Karazi when we can, working around him when we must; enhancing sub-national governance; strengthening corruption reduction efforts; and implementing a post-election compact.

  o   Afghan-led reintegration and reconciliation are essential pillars of our strategy.

  o   Principals will ensure appropriate authorities, programs and resources are in place to support a prioritized comprehensive approach.

  o   We must improve coordination of international political and economic assistance to build Afghanistan.

- Afghan-led reintegration. We must improve coordination.

This approach is not fully resourced counterinsurgency or nation building, but a narrower approach tied more tightly to the core goal of disrupting, dismantling and eventually defeating al Qaeda and preventing al Qaeda's return to safe haven in Afghanistan or Pakistan (…)."[1]

---

[1] The entire document is printed in Woodward, *Obama's Wars*, 385-390.

Annex 3: White Paper of the Interagency Policy Group's Report on U.S. Policy toward Afghanistan and Pakistan

Introduction

The United States has a vital national security interest in addressing the current and potential security threats posed by extremists in Afghanistan and Pakistan. In Pakistan, al Qaeda and other groups of jihadist terrorists are planning new terror attacks. Their targets remain the U.S. homeland, Pakistan, Afghanistan, India, Europe, Australia, our allies in the Middle East, and other targets of opportunity. The growing size of the space in which they are operating is a direct result of the terrorist/insurgent activities of the Taliban and related organizations. At the same time, this group seeks to reestablish their old sanctuaries in Afghanistan.

Therefore, the core goal of the U.S. must be to disrupt, dismantle, and defeat al Qaeda and its safe havens in Pakistan, and to prevent their return to Pakistan or Afghanistan.

The ability of extremists in Pakistan to undermine Afghanistan is proven, while insurgency in Afghanistan feeds instability in Pakistan. The threat that al Qaeda poses to the United States and our allies in Pakistan–including the possibility of extremists obtaining fissile material–is all too real. Without more effective action against these groups in Pakistan, Afghanistan will face continuing instability.

(…)

Summary of Recommendations for Afghanistan and Pakistan

(…)

Encouraging Afghan government efforts to integrate reconcilable insurgents

While Mullah Omar and the Taliban's hard core that have aligned themselves with al Qaeda are not reconcilable and we cannot make a deal that includes them, the war in Afghanistan cannot be won without convincing non-ideologically committed insurgents to lay down their arms, reject al Qaeda, and accept the Afghan Constitution.

Practical integration must not become a mechanism for instituting medieval social policies that give up the quest for gender equality and human rights. We can help this process along by exploiting differences among the insurgents to divide the Taliban's true believers from less committed fighters.

Integration must be Afghan-led. An office should be created in every province and we should support efforts by the Independent Directorate of Local Governance to develop a reconciliation effort targeting mid-to-low level insurgents to be led by provincial governors. We should also explore ways to rehabilitate captured insurgents drawing on lessons learned from similar programs in Iraq and other countries.

Annex 4: ADRP 3-07 *Stability*, Headquarters, Department of the Army, August 2012.

Disarmament, Demobilization, and Reintegration

Reintegration

3-87. Reintegration is the process through which former combatants, belligerents, and displaced civilians receive amnesty, reenter civil society, gain sustainable employment, and become contributing members of the local populace. It encompasses the reinsertion of individual former fighters and displaced civilians into host-nation communities, villages, and social groups. Reintegration is a social and economic recovery process focused on the local community. It complements other community-based programs that spur job training, employment services, and economic recovery. It includes programs to impart marketable skills to demobilized armed forces and groups, belligerents, and displaced civilians; relocation assistance to support their resettlement in civilian communities; basic and vocational education; and assistance in finding employment in local economies. It accounts for specific needs of women and children associated with armed forces and groups, as well as those of civilians forced to flee their homes after violent conflict or disaster. Reintegration also addresses the willingness of civilian communities to accept former fighters into their midst; amnesty and reconciliation are key components to successful reintegration. In this context, reintegration cannot be divorced from justice and reconciliation programs that are part of the broader transition process. Successful reintegration programs tend to be lengthy and costly, requiring the participation of multiple external and host-nation SSR actors.

3-88. Reintegration is part of the general development of a country. It leads to restoration of a national identity and a sense of citizenship and civil responsibility. Programs that genuinely reintegrate former combatants and belligerents make significant contributions economically, socially, and politically to the reconstruction of fragile states. Only through successful reintegration can a nation avoid renewed violence and instability. Reintegration inherently includes reinsertion.

3-89. The repatriation and resettlement of personnel associated with armed forces and belligerent groups involve broader political and diplomatic issues. These issues extend beyond the role of military forces but may also be integral to the reintegration process. First, reinsertion includes assistance offered to former combatants, belligerents, and displaced civilians before reintegrating. As transitional assistance, it provides basic needs of reintegrating individuals and their families. This assistance includes transitional safety allowances, food, clothes, shelter, medical services, short-term education, training, employment, and tools. While reintegration represents enduring social and economic development, reinsertion comprises short- term material and financial assistance programs intended to meet immediate needs. Second, repatriation is the return of individuals to their country of citizenship. The last issue is that resettlement relocates dislocated civilians to a third country—neither the country of citizenship nor the country into which the refugee has fled. Resettlement to a third country is granted by accord of the country of resettlement and based on a number of criteria, including legal and physical protection needs, lack of local integration opportunities, medical needs, family reunification needs, and threat of violence and torture. Note: The word "resettlement" is used in a context different from that defined in FM 3-39.40.

3-90. Military forces may establish and operate internment facilities or reintegration centers to ensure the continuity of detainee programs. Such centers established in detention centers and reintegration efforts conclude at the points of release back into society. The local populace must widely recognize, understand, and accept these and other programs that facilitate reintegration. Military forces achieve acceptance through effective inform and influence activities, utilizing Soldier and leader engagement to leverage the interaction between military forces and the local populace. Former combatants often participate in reintegration when their behavior shows some level of due process involvement links to their corrective behavior modification.

3-82. DDR efforts aim to increase the stability of the security environment by disarming and demobilizing armed forces and by helping return former combatants to civilian life. The complex DDR process has dimensions that include culture, politics, security, humanity, and socioeconomics. DDR potentially provides incentives for commanders and combatants to enter negotiations, facilitate political reconciliation, dissolve belligerent force structures, and present opportunities for former combatants and other DDR beneficiaries to return to their communities. A successful DDR program helps establish sustainable peace. A failed DDR effort can stall SSR, disrupt peace processes, and destabilize communities socially and economically. Such failure potentially leads to a renewal of conflict.

3-83. DDR aims to dismantle opposing armed groups appropriately and begin the process to shape the host nation's future security force. Typically, a DDR program transitions from disarmament and demobilization to reintegration, and as a result should be looked upon as a system. Disarmament and demobilization refers to releasing or disbanding an armed unit as well as collecting and controlling weapons and weapons systems. Reintegration refers to helping former combatants return to civilian life through benefit packages and strategies that help them socially and economically rejoin their communities. As such, both disarmament and demobilization are supporting activities to the reintegration. Effective commanders recognize that the ultimate success of DDR activities relies up successful reintegration.

Literature

ADRP 3-07 *Stability*, Headquarters, Department of the Army, August 2012.

Alexander, John, "Decomposing an Insurgency. Reintegration in Afghanistan", *RUSI Journal*, August/September 2012, Vol. 157, No. 4, 48-54.

Allen, Charles D., "Creative Thinking for Senior Leaders. An essay on creative thinking for military professionals", *US Army War College*, Carlisle, June 2013.

Alusala, Nelson, Dye, Dominique, "Reintegration in Mozambique. An unresolved affair," *ISS Paper 217*, September 2010, 1-12.

Amato, Jonathan N., "Tribes, Pashtunwali and how they impact reconciliation and reintegration efforts in Afghanistan", *Thesis submitted to the Faculty of the Graduate School of Arts and Sciences of Georgetown University in partial fulfillment of the requirements for the degree of Master of Arts in Security Studies*, Washington D.C., April 16, 2010.

Andrade, Dale, Willbanks, James H., CORDS/Phoenix, "Counterinsurgency Lessons from Vietnam for the Future," *Military Review*, March-April 2006, 9-23.

Annan, Jeannie/ Blattman Christopher/ Mazurana, Dyan/ Carlson, Khristopher , "Civil war, Reintegration, and Gender in Northern Uganda", *Journal of Conflict Resolution*, 2011. Available at the webpage:
http://www.chrisblattman.com/documents/resarch/2011.CivilWarReintegrationGender.JCR.pdf.

Aron, Raymond, *Clausewitz: Philosopher of War*, New Jersey (Prentice-Hall, Inc., Englewood Cliffs) 1985.

Asia Foundation, *Afghanistan in 2012. A Survey of the Afghan People.* Available at:
www.asiafoundation.org/resources/pdfs/surveybook2012web1.pdf (accessed April 7, 2014).

Bassford, Christopher, *Clausewitz in English. The Reception of Clausewitz in Britain and America, 1815-1945*, New York/Oxford (University Press) 1994.

Bassword, Christopher, "Clausewitz and his works" (version March 18, 2013). Available at the webpage: http://www.clausewitz.com/readings/Bassford/Cworks/Works.htm (accessed May 7, 2014).

Biddle, Stephen, "War Termination in Afghanistan," *Council on Foreign Relations*, October 29, 2013 (www.cfr.org/afghanistan/war-termination-afghanistan/p31742 (accessed May 29, 2014).

Biddle, Tami Davis, "Winston Churchill and Sir Charles Portal: Their Wartime Relationship," *Air Power Leadership: Theory and Practice*, London: The Stationary Office, 2002, 178-198.

Biddle, Tami Davis, "Grand Strategy: Art of the Possible, or Impossible Art?" *US Army War College*, Carlisle 2012.

Bliesemann de Guevara, Berit, Kuehn, Florian P., Illusion Statebuilding. Warum sich der westliche Staat so schwer exportieren laesst, Hamburg (Koerber Stiftung) 2010.

Boesche, Roger, "Kautilya's *Arthasastra* on War and Diplomacy in Ancient India," *The Journal of Military History* 67, No. 1 (January 2003): 9-37.

Boot, Max, *Invisible Armies. An Epic History of Guerrilla Warfare from Ancient Times to the Present,* New York/London (Liveright Publishing Corporation) 2013.

Boot, Max, "The Evolution of Irregular War: Insurgents and Guerrillas From Akkadia to Afghanistan," *Foreign Affairs*, 92.2 (Mar/Apr 2013), 100-114.

Brodie, Bernard, *War and Politics*, New York (Macmillan Publishing) 1973, 1-2.

Chandra, Vishal, "The Evolving Politics of Taliban. Reintegration and Reconciliation in Afghanistan", *Strategic Analysis*, Vol. 35, No. 5, September 2011, 836-848.

Clausewitz, Carl von, *On War*, edited and translated by Michael Howard and Peter Paret, Princeton/New Jersey (Princeton University Press) 1984.

Clausewitz, Carl von, "Two Notes by the Author on His Plans for Revising On war," *On War*, edited and translated by Michael Howard and Peter Paret, Princeton/New Jersey (Princeton University Press) 1984.

Carl von Clausewitz, *Der Feldzug in 1812 in Russland und die Befreiungskriege von 1813-1815*, Berlin o.J

Cleveland, Charles T., Farris, Stuart L., "Landpower", *Army*, July 2013, 20-23.

Cohen, Eliot A., *Supreme Command. Soldiers, Statesmen, and Leadership in Wartime*, New York (Anchor Books) 2003.

Combating Terrorism Center at West Point, *Letters from Abbottabad. Bin Ladin Sidelined?*, 3 May 2012 (online available: http://www2.gwu.edu) (accessed 23 October 2013).

Peter Cooper, "The Soviet Experience in Afghanistan 1978-1989, in Helmut Hammerich, Uwe Hartmann, Claus von Rosen (ed.), *Jahrbuch Innere Führung 2010. Die Grenzen des Militärischen*, Berlin 2010, 174-201.

Craig, Gordon A., *The Politics of the Prussian Army 1640-1945*, London/New York (1955/64).

Daniel, Lisa, "Reintegration builds confidence in Afghanistan," *American Forces Press Service*, 19 September 2011.

Diggins, John Patrick, *Max Weber. Politics and the Spirit of Tragedy*, New York (Basic Books 1996).

Echevarria II, Antulio J., *Toward an American Way of War*, Strategic Studies Institute, March 2004. Available at: http://www.dtic.mil/futurejointwarfare/ideas_concepts/echeverria_american_way_of_war.pdf (accessed January 20, 2014).

Freier, Nathan, "Beyond the Last War. Balancing Ground Forces and Future Challenges Risk in USCENTCOM and USPACOM", *A Report of the CSIS International Security Program,* April 2013.

Freedman, Lawrence, *Strategy. A History*, Oxford (University Press) 2013.

Gates, Robert M., *Duty. Memoirs of a Secretary at War*, New York (Alfred A. Knopf) 2014.

Gentile, Jian, "COIN is Dead: U.S. Army Must Put Strategy Over Tactics," Small Wars Journal, November 22, 2011. Available at:

http://www.worldpoliticsreview.com/articles/10731/coin-is-dead-u-s-army-must-put-strategy-over-tactics (accessed January 20, 2014).

Gerras, Stephen J., "Thinking Critically about Critical Thinking: A Fundamental Guide for Strategic Leaders," *US Army War College*, Carlisle, August 2008.

Gerras, Stephen J., Wong, Leonard, Allen, Charles D., "Organizational Culture: Applying A Hybrid Model to the U.S. Army," *US Army War College,* Carlisle, November 2008.

Larry Goodson, Thomas H. Johnson, "Parallels with the Past – How the Soviets Lost in Afghanistan, how the Americans are Losing," *Orbis*, Fall 2011, 577-599.

Gray, Colin S., „Irregular warfare: Guerrillas, insurgents and terrorists", in *War, Peace and International Relations*, London (Routledge) 2007.

Gray, Colin S., "Foreword", in: Metz, Steven, *Iraq & the Evolution of American Strategy*, Washington D.C. (Potomac Books) 2008, VII-IX.

Gray, Colin S., *Modern Strategy*, Oxford (University Press) 2012.

Gray, Colin S., *Perspectives on Strategy*, Oxford (University Press) 2013.

Hammes, T. X., "Fourth Generation Warfare Evolves, Fifth Emerges," *Military Review*, 87.3 (May/Jun 2007), 14-23.

Hanasz, Paula, "Appeasing 'upset brothers': an introduction to the Afghanistan Peace and Reintegration Program", *Australian Journal of International Affairs*, vol. 66, No. 2, April 2012, 155-168.

Hartmann, Uwe, *Carl von Clausewitz and the Making of Modern Strategy*, Potsdam (Miles-Verlag) 2002.

Heuser, Beatrice, *The Evolution of Strategy. Thinking War from Antiquity to the Present*, Cambridge (University Press) 2010.

Howard, Russell D., *Strategic Culture*, Joint Special Operations University (The JSOU Press), December 2013.

Humphreys, Macartan, Weinstein, Jeremy, "Demobilization and Reintegration", *The Journal of Conflict Resolution*, Vol. 51, No. 4 (Aug. 2007), 531-567.

Joes, Anthony James, *Resisting Rebellion. The History and Politics of Counterinsurgency*, Lexington (University Press of Kentucky) 2006.

Johnson, Mark E., "Reintegration and Reconciliation in Afghanistan. Time to end the Conflict", *Military Review*, Nov/Dec 2010, 97-101.

Jones, Seth G., "Reintegrating Afghan Insurgents." *Occasional Paper RAND National Defense Research Institute*, 2011.

Kaempf, Sebastian, „Lost through non-translation: bringing Clausewitz's writings on ‚new wars' back in", *Small Wars & Insurgencies 22*, No. 4 (October 2011), 548-573.

Paul R. Kan, "Making a Sandwich in Afghanistan: How to Assess a Strategic Withdrawal from a Protracted Irregular War", *Small Wars Journal*, February 2011, 1-13. Available at http://smallwarsjournal.com/blog/journal/docs-temp/682-kan.pdf

Kant, Immanuel, *To Perpetual Peace: A philosophical Sketch*, London (Georeg Allen&Unwin LTD.) 1917.

Kaplan, Fred, *The Insurgents. David Petraeus and the Plot to change the American Way of War*, New York/London/Toronto/ Sydney/New Delhi (Simon&Schuster) 2013.

Karsner, Christian M., Kopczynski, Sarah E., "Through and with: Reintegration in Northern Afghanistan", *Special Warfare*, 25.1 (Jan-Mar 2012), 35-43.

Kautilya, *The Artha´s-a stra,* 2nd ed., ed. and trans. R. P. Kangle, Part II of *The Kautil-tya Artha´s-astra* (Delhi: Motilal Banardisass, 1992).

Kilcullen, David, *The Accidental Guerrilla. Fighting small wars in the midst of a big one*, Oxford (University Press) 2009.

Kissinger, Henry, „The Vietnam Negotiations", in *Foreign Affairs 47*, 1969.

Kotter John P., *Leading Change*, Boston (Harvard Business Review Press) 2012.

Liddell Hart, Basil, *Strategy*, New York (Penguin Books) 1991.

Lindley, Nick, "Redpointing' Strategy: A Model for Strategy-making in Contemporary Conflict", *Royal College of Defence Studies*, July 2013.

Matyók, Thomas, Flaherty, Maureen, Tuso, Hamdesa, Senehi, Jessica, Byrne, Sean (eds.), *Peace on Earth. The Role of Religion in Peace and Conflict Studies*, Lanham (Lexington Books) 2013.

McMaster, H. R., *Dereliction of Duty. Lyndon Johnson, Robert McNamara, the Joint Chiefs of Staff, and the Lies that Led to Vietnam*, New York (Harper Perennial) 1998.

Metz, Steven, *Iraq & the Evolution of American Strategy*, Washington D.C. (Potomac Books) 2008.

Millen, Raymond A., "Time for a Strategic and Intellectual Pause in Afghanistan", *Parameters*, Summer 2010, 33-45.

Millen, Raymond A., Pruitt, Carolyn, "The Government Assistance Center: A Vehicle for Transitioning to the Host Government", *PKSOI Papers*, Carlisle, May 2011.

Morgenstein, Jonathan, Consolidating Disarmament. Lessons from Colombia's Reintegration Program for Demobilized Paramilitaries", *United States Institute of Peace*, Special Report 217 (November 2008), 1-16.

Musa, Samuel, Morgan, John, Keegan, Matt, "Policing and COIN Operations. Lessons Learned, Strategies and Future Directions," *Center for Technology and National Security Policy. The Combating Terrorism Technical Support Office*, 2011.

Nagl, John A., *Learning to eat Soup with a Knife: Counterinsurgeny Lessons from Malaya and Vietnam*, London and Chicage (University of Chicago Press) 2005.

Nordland, Rod and Rubin, Alissa J., "Taliban impostors vex reintegration plan. Many are believed to be opportunists looking for handouts", *The International Herald Tribune*, February 20, 2012.

Nye, Jr., Joseph S., Welch, David A., *Understanding Global Conflict and Cooperation. An Introduction to Theory and History*, Boston (Longman) 2011.

Özerdem, Alpaslan, Podder, Sukanya (eds.), *Child soldiers: from recruitment to reintegration*, Palgrave Macmillan 2011

Oezerdem, Alpaslan, Sofizada, Abdul Hai, "Sustainable reintegration to returning refugees in post-Taliban Afghanistan: land-related challenges", *Conflict, Security & Development*, 6:1, April 2006, 75-100.

Osgood, Robert E., *Limited War: The Challenge to American Security*, Chicago: University of Chicago Press, 1957.

Paret, Peter, *Clausewitz and the State*, Princeton/New Jersey (Princeton University Press) 1985.

Porch, Dougles, *Counterinsurgency. Exposing the Myths of the New Way of War*, Cambridge (University Press) 2013.

Parrish, Karen, "General: Afghan Reintegration Program will take time", *U.S. Department of Defense Information*, December 8, 2011.

Pellerin, Cheryl, "Afghan Insurgent Reintegration Effort Works", *U.S. Department of Defense Information*, February 22, 2012.

Phillips, P. Michael, "Deconstructing Our Dark Age Future," *Parameters*, Summer 2009, 94-110.

Pommerin, Reiner (ed.), *Clausewitz goes global. Carl von Clausewitz in the 21st Century*, Miles-Verlag (Berlin) 2011.

Rashid, Ahmed, *Descent into Chaos*, New York (Penguin) 2008.

Reid, Brian Holden, *Studies in British Military Thought*, Lincoln (University of Nebraska Press) 1998.

Robinson, Linda, *One Hundred Victories. Special Ops and the Future of American Warfare*, New York (Public Affairs): 2013.

Rosen, Claus von, "Wissenschaft und Militärische Führung in Baudissins Konzeption Innere Führung," *Jahrbuch Innere Führung 2013. Wissenschaften und ihre Relevanz für die Bundeswehr als Armee im Einsatz*, ed. by Uwe Hartmann and Claus von Rosen, Berlin 2013 (Miles-Verlag), 81-104.

Rosen, Claus von, Hartmann, Uwe, "Clausewitz and the Reception in Germany", Reiner Pommerin (ed.), *Clausewitz goes global. Carl von Clausewitz in the 21st Century*, Berlin (Miles-Verlag) 2014, 122-149.

Rumsfeld, Donald, *Known and Unknown. A Memoir*, New York (Penguin Group) 2011.

Schoux, William P., "The Vietnam CORDS Experience: A Model of successful civil-military Partnership?"; available at https://dec.usaid.gov/dec/content/Detail.aspx?q (accessed April 18, 2014).

Stoler, Mark A., *George C. Marshall. Soldier-Statesman of the American Century*, Detroit (Twayne Publishers) 1989.

Stoler, Mark A., *Allies and Adversaries: The Joint Chiefs of Staff, the Grand Alliance, and U.S. Strategy in World War II*, Chapel Hill (UNC Press) 2006.

Strachan, Hew, *The Politics of the British Army*, Oxford (University Press) 1997.

Strachan, Hew, "Strategy and contingency", *International Affairs* 87:6 (2011), 1281-1296.

Strachan, Hew, *The Direction of War*, New York (Cambridge University Press) 2013.

Streit, Christian, *Keine Kameraden, Die Wehrmacht und die sowjetischen Kriegsgefangenen 1941-1945*, Bonn (Dietz): 1997

Smith, Rupert, *The Utility of Force*, New York (Random House) 2007.

Sun Tzu, *The Art of War*. Translated and with an Introduction by Samuel B. Griffith, Oxford University Press (London/Oxford/New York) 1971.

Tamagnin, Andrea, Krafft, Teresa, "Strategic Approaches to Reintegration: Lessons Learned from Liberia", *Global Governance* 16 (2010), 13-20.

Tilly, Charles, „How War Made States and Vice Versa," *Center for Studies of Social Change, New School for Social Research*, 1987.

United Nations Inter-agency Working Group on Disarmament, Demobilization and Reintegration, *Operational Guide to the Integrated Disarmament, Demobilization and Reintegration Standards*, New York 2010.

US Department of State, *3D Planning Guide*, July 2012 (available at http://usaid.gov/sites/default/files/documents/1866/3D%20Planning%20Guide_Update_FINAL).

Weber, Max, "Politics as a Vocation," in *Weber: Selections in Translation,* ed. W. G. Runciman, trans. Eric Matthews (Cambridge: Cambridge University Press, 1978), 212–25.

Weber, Max, *Essays in Sociology*, edited by H.H. Gerth and C. Wright Mills, New York 1958.

"White Paper of the Interagency Policy Group's Report on U.S. Policy toward Afghanistan and Pakistan," March 2009 (available at http://www.whitehouse.gov/assets/documents/Afghanistan -Pakistan_White_Paper.pdf).

Woodward, Bob, *Obama's Wars*, New York/London/Toronto/Sydney (Simon&Schuster): 2010.

Xiangyu, Zeng, Chunyan, Zhang, Yufan, Zhu, "Political reconciliation in Afghanistan: progress, challenges and prospects," *Strategic Studies*, Winter 2012/Spring 2013. Available at the webpage. www.issi.org.pk/publication-files/1379480196_47959077.pdf) (accessed May 29, 2014).

Zena, Prosper Nzekani, "The Lessons and Limits of DDR in Africa," *African Security Brief*, No. 24 (Africa Center for Strategic Studies), January 2013, 1-8.

Zyk, Steven A., "Former combatant reintegration and fragmentation in contemporary Afghanistan", *Conflict, Security & Development* 9:1, April 2009, 111-131.

Acknowledgements

This book is the product of my twelve-month education as an International Fellow at the U.S. Army War College in Carlisle. The rigorous curriculum provided me with the intellectual tools needed to reflect more deeply on my experience as a staff officer assigned to the Regional Command North in Masar-e Sharif in 2012/2013. As Deputy Assistant Chief of Staff for Stability, I also dealt with the support of the Afghan reintegration program. I am very thankful to Major Tony Paulsen of the U.S. Air Force who worked at that time in my staff and with whom I intensively discussed the reintegration effort and the best ways to support it.

When I arrived in Carlisle in June 2013, I had a strong intent to reflect further on "reintegration in the midst of a war". I immediately began to read about experiences from other countries, seeking to connect the content of our curriculum's readings and discussions with this subject. I owe a debt of gratitude for intellectual stimulation to all instructors who teach at the U.S. Army War College. As a classmate of Seminar 1, I would like to extend my special gratitude to Dr. Stephen J. Gerras, Dr. Paul R. Kan, Colonel Paul M. Phillips, and Colonel Timothy D. Brown. Their classes on Strategic Leadership, Defense Management, Theory of War and Strategy, National Security Policy and Strategy, and on Theatre Strategy and Campaigning were outstanding.

I am very grateful to the Commandant of the U.S. Army War College, Major General Anthony A. Cucolo III, and to Charles D. Allen who gave me the opportunity to take part in the Commandant's Reading Program and to meet the authors Mark A. Stoler, Rick Atkinson, Linda Robinson, Andrew J. Bacevich, Robert D. Kaplan, and Eliot Cohen.

I highly appreciated the discussions in the Middle East class taught by Dr. Larry P. Goodson and in the seminar on Conflict Studies for Commanders, taught by Dr. Thomas G. Matyok. The electives on "Friction: Case Studies in Strategy, Decision-Making, and Civil-Military Relations" with Dr. Tami D. Biddle and on "Security Sector Reform" with Dr. Raymond A. Millen were extremely insightful. Ray Millen was the inspiring advisor for my Strategic Research Project that forms the main body of this book. Vielen Dank, Ray!

My special thanks go also to the International Fellows Office of the U.S. Army War College headed by Colonel John J. Burbank. Colonel Burbank and his team not only provided comprehensive support in all administrative issues but also organized trips and a negotiation exercise that provided me with brand-new experiences in policy making.

I also would like to thank those who contributed to the editing of this book: Peter Dauber, who also assisted me and my family in all regards; and Julie Nakpil Lankford, independent editor and contracted instructor of the U.S. Army War College, who did a great job in improving the wording of this book.

I would like to express my greatest appreciation for the discussions I had with my classmates in Seminar 1: Claude A. Crisp, Scott A. Green, Richard Hawkins, Chanae N. Jones, Francis Ronald Mbindi, Patrick R, Michaelis, Carl J. Packer, Mark B. Parker, John R. Pelczarski, Rob G. Picht, Jr., Keith M. Rivers, Thomas W. Singleton, John N. Tumino, Veasna Var and Jon C. Wilkinson. Thank you so much for your friendship and for sharing your experience and perspectives!

Finally, I am very grateful to my wife Carola and my children Julian and Charleen who have supported me in devoting significant time and attention to my strategic education.

Carlisle, June 6, 2014

About the Author

Uwe Hartmann is a career officer with a general staff education. He graduated from the now Helmut-Schmidt-Universität/Universität der Bundeswehr Hamburg in 1986 with a Master of Arts in pedagogy. After assignments as platoon and company commander, he returned to his alma mater as a junior lecturer in 1991. Four years later, he earned a Ph.D. in philosophy with a thesis on adult education.

Uwe Hartmann attended the General Staff course at the Command and Leadership College in Hamburg from 1995 to 1997.

In June 2001, he graduated from the National Security Affairs course at the Naval Postgraduate School in Monterey CA. 13 years later, he graduated as an International Fellow at the US Army War College in Carlisle, PA.

Uwe Hartmann has held assignments in the German Ministry of Defense, the German Parliament, in Corps headquarters, in NATO and as commander of the bi-national German-Dutch Staff Support Battalion of the I. Corps in Münster.

He served in Bosnia and Herzegovina and in Afghanistan and was part of the NATO Response Force (NRF) 4.

Uwe Hartmann has previously published books on Carl von Clausewitz and on the leadership philosophy of the German armed forces (Innere Führung). Since 2009, he has been the co-editor of the Jahrbuch Innere Führung.

He and his wife Carola, his son Julian, and his daughter Charleen live in Berlin.

Register

138

Carola Hartmann Miles-Verlag

Politik, Gesellschaft, Militär

Uwe Hartmann, *Innere Führung. Erfolge und Defizite der Führungsphilosophie für die Bundeswehr,* Berlin 2007.

Peter Heinze, *Bundeswehr „erobert" Deutschlands Osten,* Berlin 2010.

Dieter E. Kilian, *Politik und Militär in Deutschland. Die Bundespräsidenten und Bundeskanzler und ihre Beziehung zu Soldatentum und Bundeswehr,* Berlin 2011.

Hans Joachim Reeb, *Sicherheitskultur als kommunikative und pädagogische Herausforderung – Der Umgang in Politik, Medien und Gesellschaft,* Berlin 2011.

Reiner Pommerin (ed.), *Clausewitz goes global. Carl von Clausewitz in the 21ˢᵗ Century,* Berlin 2011.

Hans-Christian Beck, Christian Singer (Hrsg.), *Entscheiden – Führen – Verantworten. Soldatsein im 21. Jahrhundert,* Berlin 2011.

Ingo Pfeiffer, *Gegner wider Willen. Konfrontation von Volksmarine und Bundesmarine auf See,* Berlin 2012.

Eberhard Birk, Heiner Möllers, Wolfgang Schmidt (Hrsg.), *Die Luftwaffe zwischen Politik und Technik. Schriften zur Geschichte der Deutschen Luftwaffe, Bd. 2,* Berlin 2012.

Eberhard Birk, Winfried Heinemann, Sven Lange (Hrsg.), *Tradition für die Bundeswehr. Neue Aspekte einer alten Debatte,* Berlin 2012.

Holger Müller, *Clausewitz' Verständnis von Strategie im Spiegel der Spieltheorie,* Berlin 2012.

Angelika Dörfler-Dierken, *Führung in der Bundeswehr,* Berlin 2013.

Cornelia Fedtke, Kai-Uwe Hellmann, Jan Hörmann, *Migration und Militär. Zur Integration deutscher Soldaten mit Migrationshintergrund in der Bundeswehr,* Berlin 2013.

Torsten Konopka, *Afrikanische Wehrsysteme und ihre Entwicklung zwischen 1990/91 und 2011,* Berlin 2014.

Ingo Pfeiffer, *Seestreitkräfte der DDR,* Berlin 2014.

Wolf Graf von Baudissin, *Grundwert Frieden in Politik – Strategie – Führung von Streitkräften,* hrsg. von Claus von Rosen, Berlin 2014.

Reihe: Jahrbuch Innere Führung

Uwe Hartmann, Claus von Rosen, Christian Walther (Hrsg.), *Jahrbuch Innere Führung 2009. Die Rückkehr des Soldatischen,* Eschede 2009.

Helmut R. Hammerich, Uwe Hartmann, Claus von Rosen (Hrsg.), *Jahrbuch Innere Führung 2010. Die Grenzen des Militärischen,* Berlin 2010.

Uwe Hartmann, Claus von Rosen, Christian Walther (Hrsg.), *Jahrbuch Innere Führung 2011. Ethik als geistige Rüstung für Soldaten,* Berlin 2011.

Uwe Hartmann, Claus von Rosen, Christian Walther (Hrsg.), *Jahrbuch Innere Führung 2012. Der Soldatenberuf zwischen gesellschaftlicher Integration und suis generis-Ansprüchen,* Berlin 2012.

Uwe Hartmann, Claus von Rosen (Hrsg.), *Jahrbuch Innere Führung 2013. Wissenschaften und ihre Relevanz für die Bundeswehr als Armee im Einsatz,* Berlin 2013.

Einsatzerfahrungen

Kay Kuhlen, *Um des lieben Friedens willen. Als Peacekeeper im Kosovo,* Eschede 2009.

Sascha Brinkmann, Joachim Hoppe (Hrsg.), *Generation Einsatz, Fallschirmjäger berichten ihre Erfahrungen aus Afghanistan,* Berlin 2010.

Schwitalla, Artur, *Afghanistan, jetzt weiß ich erst… Gedanken aus meiner Zeit als Kommandeur des Provincial Reconstruction Team FEYZABAD,* Berlin 2010.

Heinz Dietrich Minkewitz, *Aus dem Tagebuch eines Nachrichtensoldaten. Mit dem Panzer-Pionierbataillon auf den Schauplätzen des Krieges,* Berlin 2014.

Erinnerungen

Blue Braun, *Erinnerungen an die Marine 1956-1996,* Berlin 2012.

Harald Volkmar Schlieder, *Kommando zurück!,* Berlin 2012.

Harald Volkmar Schlieder, *Opa Willy. 1891 Dresden – 1958 Miltenberg. Von einem, der aufsteigen wollte. Eine sächsisch-deutsche Lebensgeschichte in Frieden und Krieg,* Berlin 2012.

Harald Volkmar Schlieder, *Mein Vater – Musiker und Offizier. 1918 Dresden – 1998 Miltenberg,* Berlin 2013.

Reinhart Lunderstädt, *Aus dem Leben eines Hochschullehrers. Persönlicher Bericht,* Berlin 2012.

Wulf Beeck, *Mit Überschall durch den Kalten Krieg. Mein Leben für die Marine,* Berlin 2013.

Jan Becker, *Aufgewühltes Wasser. 3 Bde.,* Berlin 2014.

Romane

Christoph Karich, *Bewährung im Grünen Meer,* Berlin 2009.

Robert B. Thiele, *Die Treuhänderin,* Berlin 2012 (2013 als Paperback unter dem Titel „Der General" neu erschienen).

Monterey Studies

Uwe Hartmann, *Carl von Clausewitz and the Making of Modern Strategy,* Potsdam 2002.

Sven Lange, *Revolt against the West. A Comparison of the Current War on Terror with the Boxer Rebellion in 1900-01,* Berlin 2007.

Donald Abenheim, *Soldier and Politics Transformed,* Berlin 2007.

Michael G. Lux, *Innere Führung – A Superior Concept of Leadership?,* Berlin 2009.

Marc A. Walther, *HAMAS between Violence and Pragmatism,* Berlin 2010.

Frank Hagemann, *Strategy Making in the European Union,* Berlin 2010.

Ralf Hammerstein, *Deliberalization in Jordan: the Roles of Islamists and U.S.-EU Assistance in stalled Democratization,* Berlin 2011.

Ingo Wittmann, *Auftragstaktik,* Berlin 2012.

Uwe Hartmann, *War without Fighting? The Reintegration of Former Combatants in Afghanistan seen through the Lens of Strategic Thought,* Berlin 2014.

www.miles-verlag.jimdo.com